WOMEN, DECODE THE LAW OF ATTRACTION

Crack the 6 codes:

How to THINK, ACT & ATTRACT
what you really want from life!

Orly Katz, MBA
Life, Business & Career
Coach for Women

Women, Decode the Law of Attraction

Cover Design: Layani Tal, www.layanital.com
Translation: Liz Tal, Natalie Mendelsohn
Typography: Kirk Thomas, www.kirks-graphics.com

For information contact:
Creative Book Publishers International
269 S. Beverly Drive, Suite 1442, Beverly Hills, CA 90212.
www.bookpubintl.com

Library of Congress Control Number: 2007943219
Katz, Orly

Women, Decode the Law of Attraction
ISBN-13: 978-0-9779131-9-0

To my dearest beloved mother, Dalia Tal, who is also my best friend and my best coach. Thank you for being you.

Love,
Orly

"The great question that has never been answered, and which I have not yet been able to answer despite my thirty years of research into the feminine soul, is:

What does a woman want?"

— SIGMUND FREUD

CONTENTS

Introduction

I got off the train in a suburb of Frankfurt. The air was clean and refreshing, and the sky blue and cloudless. I breathed in deeply and started walking – a woman arriving alone in a strange city, sixth months pregnant, dragging a suitcase. I was headed for my hotel but saw only open farmland spreading before me. The green meadows were a beautiful sight, but I was worried about seeing no sign of human habitation. I'd been hoping, at least, for a marker pointing to the Arkaden Hotel. I took another deep breath and knew. I just knew I'd find the hotel. Every bone in my body was telling me I hadn't come there for nothing. I knew I was doing the right thing and that I'd succeed. I got one sudden sign of encouragement and reassurance: I felt kicking inside my belly. Yes, even my unborn baby believed in me. My husband's words were still echoing through my mind: "Go and show them what you have to offer. You know how good it is. You know how much it changed your own life and the lives of thousands of women. You know it works! You believe in it so much that you'll have no problem projecting it to others and ending up with exactly what you want. Go ahead. Prove, once again, that the Law of Attraction works, and that everything you wrote is right on target." And then, as if placing the final exclamation mark on his words, I heard my two children tell me, "Yeah, Mom, go for it!"

"Frankfurt Book Fair—here I come!" I walked on, still trying to convince myself that I was on the right path, literally and figuratively: "I'll find the publisher who believes in me and my book. I'll find the right publisher!" I was still deep in thought when the Arkaden Hotel suddenly appeared before me. It was very modest-looking outside, but the magic of the place struck me the moment I entered. Pink flowered curtains like those in a fairy tale cottage, embroidered carpets warming the exposed wood floor, a wood-burning fireplace emitting the scent of freshly chopped logs.

At the reception desk sat Diamantis Christoudis, the owner. He greeted me with a warm, friendly smile as if I were his long lost daughter. In broken English, he invited me to join him and his wife for a cup of coffee and some homemade cakes. Communicating mainly with sign language, Diamantis arranged a ride for me to the fair with one of the guests. I went to my room to get organized and prepare for the meetings I'd arranged. I pulled out my dainty-looking, very comfortable black suit. I took a brief glance in the mirror and was satisfied. My eyes sparkled. I saw the gleam within me. I felt the energy flowing through my veins, and I was ready to enter the meetings with confidence.

Michael was second on my list. As soon as we met, I knew I'd succeeded. I knew I'd found the publisher who would believe in me, the one who would publish the book. And that is exactly what happened. As I sit and write these lines, I still choke up with tears of excitement. The Law of Attraction has proven itself once again. Each and every one of you, dear readers, can read about it and learn it for yourselves - how to attract the reality you want into your lives, and not the reality your negative voice wants. In other words, you can learn how to become an attractive woman. Believe me - if I did it, anyone can.

The anecdotes in this book (with identifying details altered) are the real stories of women I have known, coached, and trained over the years. As you read, you will join me on a journey on which we encounter the negative voices in our lives as women and learn how to respond to them. In this way, we can apply the law of attraction and begin making ourselves attractive. We will discover what it is we consider most important and how to attract those things to our lives; we will learn about the power of thinking and its ability to generate a new reality - for ourselves and for our environment; and we will discover the connection between listening to our bodies and improving our ability to attract. All of this will serve as a booster engine as we begin to soar upward.

For you to enjoy this book and make full use of the six codes it contains, I'd like you to pamper yourselves for three hours, just three hours. Sit in a comfortable chair, make yourself a cup of hot coffee, and if anyone from your family disturbs you while you're reading, tell them you've gone on vacation for three hours. Even moms deserve that. I promise you that as you read this book you'll feel I'm speaking directly to you. You'll identify with the stories and anecdotes, laugh with me, and probably, very often, find yourself nodding in agreement.

I recommend that you keep a pencil handy to do the tips and exercises in the book and the accompanying workbook. Remember, it all depends on us, us women. We can do it if we want to! All that remains is to wish you an enjoyable and "attractive" reading experience.

Best wishes,

Orly Katz

CHAPTER 1

CRACKING CODE NO. 1 – IDENTIFICATION

So, what can we expect by cracking the first code of the Law of Attraction – The "Identification" code?

We'll learn about the Law of Attraction and how it works. We'll meet our negative voice: the NAF – our Negative Attraction Factor, that attracts what we don't want in our lives. We'll identify the dominate NAFs in our lives and meet more NAFs peculiar to women. We'll understand what we have to lose and gain when we give our NAFs center stage in our lives. We'll learn to identify when our NAF attacks us. And we'll get tips and action steps on how to cope with our NAFs and how to attract into our lives what we truly want.

The JCC auditorium in Manhattan was filled with scores of women. Everyone's ears were perked. They were eager to learn, to know how to do it – how to identify what's keeping us stuck in place and preventing us from knowing the things we really want and, most importantly, from attracting them into our lives.

A woman in her mid-40s sprang up from her chair. "Why aren't I happy? I've got a successful husband, two wonderful children, a jeep, an au pair, and a great corporate job. So why aren't I happy? Worse than that, I've lost every ounce of enthusiasm and energy. Nothing inspires or motivates me any more. I don't even know at this point what I want out of life."

"Well, I certainly know what I want," another woman responded. "I want a man - a partner, and a friend. I've had it with losers. That's the only type I attract, and they're ruining my life. I want to find love."

"And me? ... I want to fulfill my potential and change my direction and career. But I'm afraid. I don't know how to gather my courage and take that first brave step. I don't know how to attract the career I really want."

From another corner of the room, a fourth woman declared, "I just want a little peace and quiet. I want a better relationship with my children. I want a genuine relationship with my friends. I don't want to feel that people are taking advantage of me. I want to be able to say 'no' and to feel okay about it."

I looked at all the women sitting in my workshop. Women just like you and me. Each one with her own life story. Each knowing where she came from and knowing that she wanted to change, initiate, dare, and add some spices to her life in order to live it fully and not only view it from the sidelines. The problem was they didn't know what spices to add.

"If we live our lives within the echo of the negative voices in our heads and we don't allow ourselves to grow, develop, or make the changes we need to make," I opened, "then we are not really living. We merely exist. We don't attract to our lives the things we truly desire but only what we don't want; meaning, in one sense at least, that we're not 'attractive'."

Everything is a matter of choice. We choose the reality of our lives. The six codes teach us how to make conscious use of the Law of Attraction in order to attract positive opportunities and create the reality we desire. We can get more of what we want out of life and less of what we don't want; in short, we can live the lives we've always desired, rather than merely glimpsing at them occasionally while too often we let the negative voices dictate the rules.

"I don't believe in magic," one woman responded.

"I'm with you!" I answered her. "There's no hocus-pocus or sleight of hand here. It's intensive work and coaching. It's learning about the six codes that will bring you, slowly but surely, to the place you'd like to be. It's about discovering the six codes that become your tools for coping and for identifying and choosing what is good for you. You may not see the light immediately. But with the tools you get, you'll learn how to identify the opportunity when it does arrive. You'll know how to grab it with both hands. The six codes will help you define your current situation, identify what needs improvement, and isolate the negative voices. And, of course, everything you do here will relate directly to your real life. But enough talking. Let's get to work!"

What is the Law of Attraction and how does it work?

Have you ever noticed how sometimes things work out for the best, just as you'd hoped and expected – like a hand in a glove or a perfect fit for that missing puzzle piece? All of a sudden, you meet the ideal client, The one you've been dreaming about. Or you just got that phone call you've been anxiously awaiting, offering you the job of a lifetime. Or you met a knight in shining armor (a real flesh-and-blood one), and to top things off he's entranced with you, too. And all that happened, in your humble opinion, because you were in the right place at the right time. Well, that's not how it works. The real explanation rests in the Law of Attraction.

Is the opposite situation also familiar to you, the one in which you attract the same types of people and events into your life, even if they do you no good? They may be partners who make your life miserable, girlfriends who aren't your type, unsatisfying jobs, a daily routine you'd be better off without…

According to the Law of Attraction, we attract the things we want as well as the things we'd rather avoid! In practical terms, it's the vibes we transmit to others – both positive and negative – that determine what we attract to ourselves. A negative voice creates negative vibes that we send out to our environment, and, in the end, these vibes attract into our lives the things we do not want. A positive voice, however, creates positive vibes that attract what we do want and long for. For better or for worse, both types of vibes create the reality in which we live.

The Law of Attraction reacts to what we think and broadcast by giving us back - whether good or bad - more of what we think and broadcast. Each and every one of us projects or conveys something. Consider the statement, "She projects positive energy, positive vibes."

If you're excited, satisfied, in love, elated, you project it - your vibes are positive. But what if your negative voices are holding the reins? What happens when you're angry or frightened? When you feel inferior your conscience nags you. You lose your confidence and you feel like a miserable victim. You'll probably project those feelings, emit those bad vibes, and transmit that negative energy - even subconsciously.

It's important that you be aware of what you project and what you feel. The vibes emanating from you are what determine your Law of Attraction - what, in the end, you attract into your own life: good or bad, positive or negative…

The following anecdote perfectly illustrates the Law of Attraction:

Maria's Story (source unknown)

Maria Guadalupe lived with her mother in a small apartment on Manhattan's Upper West Side. Maria was not young but not old. Not short but not tall. She wasn't thin but wasn't fat. Not particularly beautiful but not ugly. Not overly intelligent but no dummy. Maria Guadalupe was an average woman. She worked as a menial office worker in a large company and her life was gray, routine and boring. There were people at work, the few who noticed she existed, who would say that Maria herself was gray, routine and boring.

One morning, on the way to work, Maria noticed a new hat store in the neighborhood. A sudden flash of curiosity and naughtiness swept through her, the kind she felt long ago when she was a child. The next moment she was inside the store. A mother and her young daughter were inside, picking out a hat for the girl. Another woman was eyeing the merchandise for herself. Maria walked around the store and, bashfully, tried on a few hats. Then, one hat sitting at the end of the top shelf drew her attention. Maria tried it on, and... it suited her! The first one to notice was the little girl. She pulled on her mother's sleeve and said, "Mommy, mommy, look at that pretty woman in the hat!" The mother couldn't help but walk over to Maria to say, "You know, that hat really suits you!" The other customer overheard her and came over to offer her own compliment: "You really do look very pretty in that hat. It's just *you*."

Maria walked over to the large mirror, looked at her image and for the first time in her adult life liked the way she looked. With eyes aglow and a smile spread across her lips, she went to the cashier, paid for the hat, and left the store.

Outside, a new world was awaiting her. She'd never before noticed the flower arrangements along the sidewalk, or the fresh air around her. The noise of traffic and pedestrians blended like harmonious music. She felt like she was floating, her heart buoying her up with gladness.

When she passed a café that was on her morning route she noticed the regular customers sitting at their usual tables. One of the nicer looking young men there lifted his eyes from his newspaper and called to her: "Hey darling, you look good! Are you new around here? Can I invite you for a cup of coffee?" Maria blushed and continued on her merry way.

When she got to her office building, the guard opened the door and greeted her with a "Good Morning." He'd never done that before. The people in the elevator asked her what floor she wanted and pressed the button for her. Her coworkers seemed to notice her for the first time. Everyone mentioned the sparkle in her eyes and complimented her on how pretty she looked. Later, her departmental manager invited her to lunch on the pretense that it had been a long time since they discussed how she feels about her job. To her amazement, he started flirting with her during lunch.

When her enchanted working day ended, Maria decided, for a change of pace, to take a taxi home. Before she even raised her hand to flag one down, two taxis pulled over. She entered one, sat in the back seat, and reflected on the wonderful day that had just passed and how her life had changed because of the hat she bought.

When she got to her apartment building, she flew up the stairs and rang the bell. Her mother opened the door and stood there speechless. When she managed to catch her breath, she said, "Maria, how nice you look! Your eyes are sparkling, just like when you were a little girl."

"I know, mother," said Maria. "It's all because of the hat."

Her mother looked at her and asked, "Maria, what hat?"

Maria raised her hand to her head in horror and discovered what she truly feared had happened. The hat that had changed her life was no longer there. She sank into the couch and recalled the events of the day, hour after hour. She had to know how she'd lost the magical hat. She didn't remember taking it off in the taxi, at lunch, at work, in the elevator, or on the street. She replayed the scene of entering the store, noticing the hat on the shelf, placing it on her head, looking into the mirror, walking to the cashier to pay, and, yes, clearly and painfully now, placing the hat on the counter while she took out her wallet, and forgetting to take it when she left.

Oh my, Maria. And oh my, all of us. If we only believed, all the time, that we were pretty, smart, and successful, that is what we'd be. After all, that is, indeed, the Law of Attraction.

To maximize this phenomenon, to live the reality we've always dreamed of, we must activate Code No. 1 - the Code of Identification:

First we must identify our current situation and where we need to make changes and improvements. We must identify the negative voices that prevent us from attracting into our lives what we desire. We must identify the vibes we send out at any given moment. And, of course, we must identify the reality best suited to us, the one we would like to live and attract into our lives.

It's Not You, Its Your NAF

- How many times have you tossed and turned, unable to sleep, reliving that unsuccessful conversation you had today, angry with yourself about the things you said, or didn't say?

- How many times have you conceded, given up, and not continued in the direction you really wanted to, just because you thought you wouldn't succeed or weren't good enough?

- How many times have you said "Yes" when you really wanted to say "No," just because you felt awkward?

- How many times have you stood in front of that mirror, examining all your physical "imperfections," and tortured yourself about them all day, and the day after?

Does that sound familiar? How many of those thoughts go through our heads every day and refuse to give us a moment's peace, even at night when we try to fall asleep? How much of each day is occupied by these negative thoughts rushing around in our brains, confusing us, undermining us, and stopping us? Keeping us from attracting positive things into our lives - things we really want, dream about, long for? Isn't it time to put an end to it all? How much longer can we wear out our brains with so many exhausting thoughts? There is a way to silence that negative voice we all know so well, the one that constantly echoes in our brain. We can turn things around and begin to take control of our lives. We can attract what we want and are interested in, and not what our negative voices dictate to us.

Meet the NAF, our Negative Attractive Factor. Our NAF is our negative voice that leads us to attract into our lives what we do not want and what is not good for us. The NAF creates our current situation and prevents us from changing it to one we truly desire. In short, it keeps us from being attractive! How does it do this? The NAF instills us with fear, and, as a result, determines the vibes we send out. The most dominant of these vibes are negative vibes, the ones that eventually attract the things we don't want in our lives.

I'm not talking about merely one voice that threatens us. There's a whole chorus of negative voices singing within us, and we listen to them with our eyes shut. The amazing thing is how easy it is for us to get lost inside our negative voices. We fail to even recognize them as negative. We believe that our faults and inabilities are innate weaknesses and character flaws. Why don't we listen to our positive, optimistic voices in the same unquestioning way?

The most important part of coping with the negative voice in our lives is the understanding that this voice is not us! It's just a particular voice inside us, one of many. Yet even though it's only one of our voices, it silences the other ones to the point where we can no longer hear them. All our negative voices combine into a single, very convincing dominant voice and we behave according to its demands. We send out negatives vibes, and... yes, we attract what we don't want into our lives.

To return to a balanced state, we'll need to re-separate ourselves from our negative voice and learn to listen to the other voices echoing within us – the optimistic ones that, over time, were pushed aside and disappeared.

Think of it as a zipper. Today it's closed – we're attached to our negative voice as one unit. Our objective is to open the zipper to separate the two individual halves. We are one entity and our negative voice is another separate entity. Once we have separated the two parts from each other, we can develop an awareness of the very existence of our negative voice. We can recognize it, observe it from a distance, and relate to the whole matter with less identification and less emotional involvement. And most importantly, we can begin to release ourselves from the control of our negative voice. We can turn the tide and begin to take control of our own lives. We can attract what we are interested in and most desire, not what our negative voice dictates to us.

Remember: We attract into our lives everything that we're thinking about, focusing on, and emphasizing (good or bad, positive or negative.) The Law of Attraction responds to the vibes we send out by giving us back more of the same, for better or for worse.

Imagine the following scenario: You've recently divorced and you're interested in meeting someone new. A nice guy who could become your new life partner. Someone fond of your children, attentive to your needs. All in all, someone who'll make your life pleasurable rather than miserable.

Option A: Your NAFs are echoing through your mind: "There's no way you're going to find a man. You always attract the ones you don't want. You'll never succeed in a relationship." Frustrated, you say, half-moaning, "I want to find a man."

Option B: You're sending out positive vibes of excitement and anticipation. According to the Law of Attraction, you will attract men – many men – regardless of your outward appearance. And of all of them, you'll be able to choose the one you want!

The reason, in either case, is very simple. We attract to our lives what we focus on, think about, and believe in – for better or for worse. That's the Law of Attraction.

To Each Her Own NAF

And now, I've got news for you. Each and every one of us has a NAF. But each of us has her personal, particular type of NAFs. As you probably know, that "asset" does not belong to women alone. Our friends, men, suffer from NAFs to the same degree. But their types are male NAFs, and that's the subject of another book...

Our NAF has a many-branched, hopelessly tangled family tree, consisting of generations of NAFs – brothers, sisters, cousins, grandparents, you name it. Each of these NAFs has a name and specific function. Each specializes in a particular kind of bullying.

There's a NAF responsible for our fear of stating our opinions publicly. It echoes through our head and tells us that the minute we say what we think, people will make fun of us, get angry, or become hurt. After that NAF says what it has to say, we actually attract these undesirable situations into our lives. It's true, our expectations come true.

There's a NAF responsible for the suffering our outward appearance causes us. It tells us constantly that we're fat, that we've gotten old, and that we're not attractive. There's a NAF responsible for our fear of illness. It tells us that every doctor's visit will bring on a catastrophe.

And on and on. The list continues...

What are your NAFs?

Questionnaire: Recognizing your Dominant NAFs

I've prepared a questionnaire with 60 familiar statements to help you recognize your dominant NAFs. Read the following statements and decide how true they are for you.

How often does the statement describe your situation?

(0) never, (1) rarely, (2) sometimes, (3) always

This questionnaire is for you, so be honest in your answers.

1. I look at myself in the mirror and find new blemishes or wrinkles.

   (0) (1) (2) (3)

2. I have to know everything, right now.

   (0) (1) (2) (3)

3. Deep down inside, I feel I'm worthless.

   (0) (1) (2) (3)

4. When I have a problem, I say to myself in desperation, "What have I done to deserve this?"

   (0) (1) (2) (3)

5. I put other people's interests before my own.

   (0) (1) (2) (3)

6. I am afraid of uncertainty and instability.

   (0) (1) (2) (3)

7. I feel a need to be perfect.

   (0) (1) (2) (3)

8. If my (or my family's) source of income is threatened, I feel like it's the end of the world.

   (0) (1) (2) (3)

9. I consider my partner's career to be more important than my own, and sacrifice my career for his.

   (0) (1) (2) (3)

10. I am deeply disturbed by the feeling that I don't do enough for my children.

    (0) (1) (2) (3)

11. I feel that everyone is "out to get me."

    (0) (1) (2) (3)

12. I am afraid to tell other people when I'm feeling good, in case something bad happens.

    (0) (1) (2) (3)

13. I feel that other people are more successful than I am.

    (0) (1) (2) (3)

14. I go over conversations in my head and consider all the things I should or should not have said.

    (0) (1) (2) (3)

15. My "to do list" haunts me, and I cannot rest until everything gets done.

    (0) (1) (2) (3)

16. I remember nostalgically what I looked like when I was younger.

    (0) (1) (2) (3)

17. Before engaging in a stressful activity, the vision in my head is one of failure and not success.

    (0) (1) (2) (3)

18. I feel guilty whenever I say "No."

    (0) (1) (2) (3)

19. I get depressed when I can't close the top button of my pants.

    (0) (1) (2) (3)

20. It bothers me if someone else is more successful than I am.

    (0) (1) (2) (3)

21. Fear of losing money prevents me from doing things I really want to do.

    (0) (1) (2) (3)

22. If I know I'm right in an argument or a difference of opinion, it is very important to me that everyone else know I'm right.

    (0) (1) (2) (3)

23. I constantly push my children to achieve.

    (0) (1) (2) (3)

24. I get stressed out before a visit to the doctor.

    (0) (1) (2) (3)

25. I don't want my girlfriends to know how much money I have.

    (0) (1) (2) (3)

26. I am jealous of women my age who have advanced in their careers while successfully raising a family.

    (0) (1) (2) (3)

27. I always concentrate on negative aspects, even when positive aspects far outweigh them.

    (0) (1) (2) (3)

28. I am my own biggest critic.

    (0) (1) (2) (3)

29. I am never happy with my appearance.

    (0) (1) (2) (3)

30. To the greatest degree possible, I avoid starting new things, or changing existing things, for fear of failure.

    (0) (1) (2) (3)

31. I always listen to other people's criticism and take it seriously.

    (0) (1) (2) (3)

32. I constantly correct things I've already done so they'll be perfect.

    (0) (1) (2) (3)

33. I wake up in the middle of the night panicking about money.

    (0) (1) (2) (3)

34. It annoys me when other people don't do what I think they should.

    (0) (1) (2) (3)

35. I am always beset with worry about my children.

    (0) (1) (2) (3)

36. I think that every unusual pain or feeling in my body is a sign of some terrible illness.

    (0) (1) (2) (3)

37. I say "touch wood" whenever I tell anyone about something good, or relate some good news.

    (0) (1) (2) (3)

38. I can never completely enjoy myself, since I always find a reason to be worried/dissatisfied/uneasy.

    (0) (1) (2) (3)

39. My conscience bothers me every time I eat something sweet.

    (0) (1) (2) (3)

40. Fear that I won't finish something on time sends me into a frenzy of activity or a state of paralysis.

    (0) (1) (2) (3)

41. I feel that professionally I am capable of much more, but I lack initiative.

    (0) (1) (2) (3)

42. I get really upset if someone is dissatisfied with me.

    (0) (1) (2) (3)

43. Large or unexpected expenses stress me out.

    (0) (1) (2) (3)

44. I am very aware of each extra pound I gain.

    (0) (1) (2) (3)

45. I feel that I am not a good enough mother.

    (0) (1) (2) (3)

46. I find it hard to come to terms with my weaknesses.

    (0) (1) (2) (3)

47. I panic before a new assignment.

    (0) (1) (2) (3)

48. In my heart of hearts, I am always waiting for someone to "get me out of this mess."

    (0) (1) (2) (3)

49. My fear of failure makes me constantly change direction and prevents me from concentrating on one thing at a time.

    (0) (1) (2) (3)

50. I avoid visiting hospitals.

    (0) (1) (2) (3)

51. It is very important to me that everything go according to plan.

    (0) (1) (2) (3)

52. If people tell me I look good, I never really believe them.

    (0) (1) (2) (3)

53. I am fed up of being at home, but no one will hire me now, at my age, with no experience.

    (0) (1) (2) (3)

54. I am always trying new diets, but nothing helps.

    (0) (1) (2) (3)

55. I am afraid of the evil eye.

    (0) (1) (2) (3)

56. I always see the half empty glass.

    (0) (1) (2) (3)

57. I give up after a failure and do not carry on and try again.

    (0) (1) (2) (3)

58. It stresses me out to hear about other people's illnesses.

    (0) (1) (2) (3)

59. It is very important to me that other people do not view me as self-centered.

    (0) (1) (2) (3)

60. I feel helpless.

    (0) (1) (2) (3)

PATIENCE!!!

We will soon get to the Key to the Questionnaire…

But first, now that everything is out in the open (including the things we don't really like to talk or think about) let's take a minute to read the **"Official NAF Guide"** and familiarize ourselves with the most popular women's NAFs.

The guide includes the dominant NAFs most prevalent in women, but the list is endless, and you are welcome to add your own only-too-familiar NAFs!

After you've read the guide, you can use the Key to the Questionnaire to identify your own dominant NAFs and see how they affect your ability to attract what's really important to you.

The Official NAF Guide

1. Failure NAF

Failure NAF prevents us from making changes. Its objective is to make sure that we remain in the same place. This NAF makes us fear failure and reminds us of our previous failures. It discourages us from trying because it's obvious we will never succeed.

It has two brothers: **Perfectus NAF,** and **Worthless NAF.**

Perfectus NAF makes us believe that everything we do has to be perfect. Yet at the same time, it manages to convince us that nothing we do is good enough. This disparity creates strong feelings of anger, makes us disappointed in ourselves, and discourages us from starting new projects.

Worthless NAF constantly reminds us that we are worth nothing and prevents us from recognizing our own value. It is this NAF that makes us continually compare ourselves to others and realize that we will never "measure up."

2. "What Will They Say?" NAF

This **NAF** stops us from doing what we really want to do, and saying what we really think, for fear of criticism and negative reactions from people around us. We are scared of "what they will say."

His cousin, **Please Everybody NAF,** plays a key role.

Please Everybody NAF makes us pass up what we really want, and it ensures that everybody else around us gets what they want, at our expense, Just because we are afraid to appear self-centered.

3. Half Empty Glass NAF

This NAF reminds us to see the negative aspects of every situation. It prevents us from enjoying the good things that happen to us and keeps on pointing out the bad points about everything. It wakes up every time we begin to feel that little spark of satisfaction or happiness, and it makes sure we are never satisfied and never allow ourselves any pleasure or tranquility.

4. *Hypochondriac NAF*

This NAF convinces us that every physical abnormality we (or one of our family members) experience, is a sign of a fatal illness. It makes us quake with fear when we see the slightest spot or bruise or when we have a fever or lose weight. Every time we go to the doctor, even for a routine checkup, it's there, lurking in the shadows with dire predictions about the test results.

Its cousin, **Malignant NAF**, is an expert on cancer. It constantly reminds us that we are only guests in this world, and that sooner or later, we, or one of our beloved family members, will be stricken with that most terrible fate. It encourages us to listen to other people's horror stories about illness and reminds us to be alert, because our time will come...

5. *Uglybug NAF*

Uglybug NAF is there every time we look in the mirror and it never fails to remind us how awful we look. It has two disciples that follow it faithfully.

Fatso NAF, which is always around to remind us how fat we are, and how we should be on a permanent diet. It sends us on a guilt trip every time we taste something sweet, or if, by some chance, we can't quite close the top button on our pants. On the other hand, if we do actually start that diet, it always pops up to tempt us to "taste just a little bit..."

Wrinkly NAF reminds us of our advanced age and points out all of those little lines on our faces. It arouses those negative thoughts about our appearance every time we look in the mirror, especially before we meet our girlfriends for lunch or get ready for a night out - in other words every time we need to look our best.

6. "What Have I Done to Deserve This?" NAF

"What Have I Done to Deserve This?" **NAF** always makes sure that we see ourselves as the underdog. It makes us feel like helpless victims. *"What have I done to deserve this? It always happens to me…"* It convinces us that other people are responsible for our suffering, cultivates a lack of faith in our ability to help ourselves, and leads us to believe that only someone else can save us.

7. Controllus NAF

Controllus NAF stimulates our need for control – over our children, our partner, our future. Without it nothing will work out, nothing will go right. It instills us with constant uncertainty and fear about the future. It equates change with instability.

Its cousin, known as **Pressure NAF**, constantly reinforces our *"Right Now"* attitude. We have to know everything, *"right now,"* and we must have results *"right now."* It infuses us with a fear that we will never manage to do everything we have to do, thereby creating a state of either frenzied activity or frozen paralysis.

8. Kiddimus NAF

Kiddimus NAF stimulates our worries, guilt feelings, and pangs of conscience in all matters connected with our children. It niggles us day and night, and reminds us that we are inadequate mothers and don't do enough for our children.

9. Careeristus NAF

Careeristus NAF persists in pointing out our missed opportunities – in our careers, professional lives, and attempts at self-fulfillment. It reminds us that we are "wasted" in what we are doing now, or that we are just not good enough in our profession – but, of course, it's too late to do anything about that now!

10. Money, Money, Money NAF

Money, Money, Money NAF constantly drums into us the fear of having no money, or the consequences of not having enough money.

It makes us feel like the end of the world is near if our source of income is threatened, or if we have a sudden or especially large expense.

11. Evil Eye NAF

Evil Eye NAF prevents us from sharing with others the good things that happen in our lives, and it prevents us from being proud of ourselves, our children, and our achievements because, obviously, something bad is bound to happen if we tell the wrong people. It also stops us from rewarding ourselves for our achievements and from enjoying ourselves and being happy, for fear that something bad might happen.

Stop a minute, and think! Do you have another "pet NAF" that isn't included in this list?

And now, the moment we've all been waiting for! Having familiarized ourselves with all the different categories of NAF with the aid of the **Official NAF Guide**, the Key to the Questionnaire will help each one of us understand which are our most dominant NAFs.

How to Recognize Your Dominant NAF

Questionnaire Key:

NAF	Questions	Number of Points for Each Question	Total Number of Points (see below)
Uglybug NAF/ Wrinkly NAF	1, 16, 29, 52		
Half Empty Glass NAF	14, 27, 38, 56		
Please Everybody NAF	5, 18, 42, 59		
Worthless NAF	3, 13, 28, 31		
Failure NAF	17, 30, 49, 57		
Perfectus NAF	7, 20, 32, 46		
Money, Money, Money NAF	8, 21, 33, 43		
Controllus NAF	6, 22, 34, 51		
Kiddimus NAF	10, 23, 35, 45		
Hypochondriac NAF	24, 36, 50, 58		
Evil Eye NAF	12, 25, 37, 55		
Careeristus NAF	9, 26, 41, 53		
"What have I done to Deserve This?" NAF	4, 11, 48, 60		
Pressure NAF	2, 15, 40, 47		
Fatso NAF	19, 39, 44, 54		

Key:

Let's use the Evil Eye NAF as an example. If you answered Question 12 - (2), Question 25 – (3), Question 37 – (1) and Question 55 – (2), the total number of points is: 2 + 3 + 1 + 2 = 8.

The Three Dominant NAFs:

Which three **NAFs** scored the most points?

1. _____

_____

2. _____

_____

3. _____

_____

These are your "**Dominant NAFs.**"

And what about the rest? Any **NAF** that scored six or more points is a "NAF To Watch Out For." Keep an eye on it, and on how it affects you.

Important Note:

You must remember that a "NAF Attack" may be dependent on external factors. There can be times in your life when a certain NAF (or its relatives) dominates your life, while at other times you might be influenced by entirely different NAFs. For example, a woman whose husband is out of work might suffer from the **Money, Money, Money NAF**, but then as soon as her husband finds a job it will no longer affect her.

What Drives Your NAF?

In the same way that food sustains human life and fuel drives a car, our thoughts are food for our NAF. They nourish it, and it grows and blossoms since we think about every little thing – dwell on it and analyze it.

Our NAF is just waiting for an opportunity, even a little crack, a slight hesitation or fear... and it immediately springs into action. The more attention we pay, the stronger it becomes. Our NAF looks for fertile ground and lays down roots immediately.

Even though we feel its negative effects today, our NAF developed way back in our childhood, with one purpose – to protect us. The NAF was created to warn us about anything, even the smallest little thing, That could possibly threaten us. It might be the fear of being left alone, the need for love, or a deep-seated fear of criticism. It works as hard as it can to prevent these things from happening to us. But, realistically speaking, there is a difference between what our NAF thinks is good for us and what we ourselves really want.

Our NAF regards us as scared little girls, and it reacts like a ferocious guard dog. But now that we are grown up, we are strong enough to dare to take chances, and the NAF's over-protectiveness is counterproductive.

Eventually the tables are turned. Instead of the NAF acting as a protector, it suddenly takes control and starts to fill our heads with endless worries and imaginary negative thoughts about things that might happen, even disasters. It doesn't allow us a moment's peace; and since it knows us even better than our own mothers do, it uses manipulations and pretexts that it knows will influence and convince us. It succeeds in hitting each and every one of us in our weakest spot with the things that bother us and upset us most.

Let's take the example of Rachel. Rachel wants to look for a job. After having two children and staying at home with them for a while, Rachel wants to get out of the house and find a job in her profession.

She feels wasted at home, and it is very important to her to put her skills to use. But whenever Rachel starts to look for a job, her NAF jumps up and reminds her that whatever job she finds will be at the expense of her children and her family. Rachel's NAF recognizes her weak spot – her need to be available to her children at all times – and continually plays on her guilt feelings. In the end, Rachel stops looking for a job and remains frustrated, both professionally and personally, by her continued lack of self-fulfillment.

Identify What Vibes You're Sending Out?

The Law of Attraction operates in our lives whether or not we're aware of it, and whether or not we want what it brings. Until we learn how to use the Law of Attraction deliberately, according to the six codes described in this book, we'll be attracting the things we devote most of our mental energy thinking about.

We're now going to try and use the Law of Attraction to its maximum effect in order to deliberately attract what we want. That is, we will decide what we want to attract to our lives and what we do not. To accomplish this, we must first be aware of the messages and vibes we're projecting outward.

If you're curious about what you are radiating to your surroundings in any specific area of your life, all you have to do is take a good look at that area and assess what you've accomplished. How satisfied are you with what you discover? If the answer is "not very," you've probably let your NAFs take control and call the shots. As a result, you've been sending out negative vibes, and the inevitable result is that you've been attracting undesirable results. The opposite is true if your assessment was positive. The results, good or bad, are in direct correlation with the Law of Attraction!

Identify what you've got to gain and lose by letting your NAF have center stage

In order to cope with our NAF and attract the reality we want, we must begin with a very important assumption – the choice is in our hands! We are the ones to decide how our lives will look. If things are bad, it's because we chose to listen to our NAF. And if things are good, it's because we chose to go our own route! Everything is a matter of choice. If things are going badly in a particular area of our lives, it's because we chose to turn our attention to some other area. That raises the question of why we continue to listen solely and blindly to our NAF even though we know what damage is caused when we heed its words. We know we attract undesirable situations of worry, anxiety, or fear. Yet we persist in heeding the NAF. The answer to the question is very simple. Behind every loss there's a gain. And that gain is the instrument played by our NAF to woo us into abiding by what it says. Even if the gain is sub-conscious, it is what causes us to choose to invest our efforts in one area and not another. This gain prevents us, in the end, from attracting what is good for us in every aspect of our lives.

Hidden in every activity we perform, or do not perform, is a gain/loss situation. To deal with our NAF, we must consciously identify our gain and loss in every situation. Which is greater? Only then, when we see the two options before us, and not only the negative one etched by our NAF, can we make an objective decision and begin to act. The loss is clear to us. But only when we're able to understand the gain as well, we will we see the full picture.

Rhonda's Story

Rhonda was an attractive woman in her late 30s. She had a stellar career, a supportive family, and a wide circle of friends. But she had one Achilles' heel – relationships. Rhonda was not able to find a partner with whom she could share her life and raise a loving family. The *one-and-only* had yet to make an appearance, and Rhonda entered a long period of frustration. For years, she tried finding someone on the Web, went on blind dates arranged by her friends, and checked out the prospects at work. But all was in vain. Her **Failure NAF** declared that she'd never find what she was looking for, and her **"What Have I Done to Deserve This?" NAF** made her feel like a helpless victim.

This was Rhonda's life, and before she knew it she was brushing up against age 40. That was when, on top of all the other voices in her head, the call of the stork began to sound, heralding the arrival of the **Ticking Clock NAF.** It rang in her ears day and night. It was telling her that if she waited any longer, she'd miss the opportunity to experience motherhood by giving birth to her own baby. It reminded her that time was not working in her favor, and that every passing moment was bringing her one step away from becoming pregnant. Rhonda decided to take action and break out of the vicious cycle she'd entered. That's when she came to me for a few coaching conversations in which we identified how satisfied she was with various aspects of her life.

And then, after she'd examined and assessed all the different aspects of her life, we saw that she'd given the lowest scores to partnership and motherhood. Rhonda was not surprised, since it was clear to her that no partner was about to turn up, and motherhood seemed further away than ever. I decided to ask her what she might be gaining by these two situations. In her estimation, her endless search for the perfect partner gave her the illusion that perhaps, in the end, she would find the person she was looking for, with no compromises.

When I asked what she might be gaining by not fulfilling her desire for motherhood, Rhonda stopped to think for a while. She responded by saying that she was, essentially, preserving her freedom. She was independent, spiritually and economically, and she could devote herself to her career. So, I asked her why these two aspects of her life continued to nag her, and why she still wanted to fulfill them. Rhonda was quite frank in her answer: she was not willing to give up the idea of bringing her own child into the world. I persisted and asked her what else she had to gain by not becoming a mother. After another pause, Rhonda answered that she was gaining the possibility of still finding the man with whom she would like to have a child, a full-time partner for both her and her child. The other possibility would be to shut herself off from any prospective partner for the next two years, thus closing the door on any chance for a conventional family.

This is where our conversation changed course. Rhonda identified her two dominant NAFs. She saw how they were related directly to her dissatisfaction with these two very important aspects of her life, and she understood how they kept her from acting by making her well aware of the benefits that each one brought. Rhonda realized how her NAFs were causing her to project negative vibes that drew her into a reality she did not desire, one without a partner and without a child.

Rhonda decided, indeed, To act. She understood that it all depended on her and the priorities she set for herself. She determined that the most important thing in her life at the moment was to fulfill her desire for motherhood, before it was too late, and she opted to become a single parent. She knew she'd be able to find a partner later, even with a child in tow. Her NAFs calmed down, and, miracles of miracles, before long Rhonda had attracted the situation she wanted; she became pregnant.

Identify when your NAF is on the attack?

In order to effectively implement Code No. 1, the **Identification Code**, we have to identify our NAF as soon as it begins to attack, and not when we are already in the grip of our NAFs.

But how do we know exactly when our NAF is attacking us?

Have you ever felt how a headache starts off and builds up? Or felt a pain in your chest that radiates throughout your body? What about that quickening heartbeat or profound sweating? No, I'm not talking about a heart attack, heaven forbid. I'm talking about the physical symptoms we feel when our NAF attacks us.

Do you ever feel deep-seated anger, fear, depression, or frustration? And, again, I'm not talking about a terrible disaster but about the feelings that hit us when our NAF attacks.

Do you recognize that feeling of helplessness and indecision – basically the feeling that you're "stuck?" This is the sense of paralysis we feel when our NAF attacks us.

And finally – what about terrible dreams and nightmares that attack us in the middle of the night? Are you ever unable to fall asleep? Or do you wake up at dawn, staring at the ceiling, which stares blankly back at you but does nothing to calm the havoc your NAF has wreaked.

As you can see, this is no laughing matter. Our NAF is very conscientious, and when it attacks us it pours all its energies into the job.

Action Steps — Surveillance!

Just as calorie counting helps us to follow a diet and lose weight, surveillance of our NAF's thoughts helps us to keep it in check.

Over the next week, note carefully exactly how many times each one of your NAFs attacks you, and exactly what it says to you.

The very fact that you are aware of your NAF and its behavior encourages the Identification process.

NAF:_____

What it says: _____

When it attacks: _____

NAF:_____

What it says: _____

When it attacks: _____

NAF:_____

What it says: _____

When it attacks: _____

NAF:_____

What it says: _____

When it attacks: _____

And now, as promised, my tips for Code No. 1 – The Identification Code

The tips at the end of each chapter are a "first aid kit." I've chosen tips that have been most helpful to the women that I've worked with.

Tip 1 – Pinch me – or, How can you stop your NAF right from the start?

A powerful way to counter your NAF's attacks is to exchange the emotional pain for physical pain. What do I mean? Every time you feel your NAF raring to attack, pinch yourself until it hurts. Yes, really pinch yourself! That pinch causes you physical pain, which awakens you, in a very concrete fashion, to the emotional pain your NAF is causing you. It's a kind of stop sign with a clear message: No more! You are in control, not your NAF. You, rather than your NAF, will decide what you want to attract into your life. You'll be amazed to see how effective this simple technique can be.

Tip 2 – How can you listen and talk to your NAF?

Sometimes your NAF is so strong that it holds you back and stops you from fulfilling your goals. When this happens, it is absolutely impossible to ignore your NAF. A strong NAF will protect you with all its might. It worries about you and fears for you. Now is the time to stop and really listen to it. Don't be sidetracked by the superficial things it says as it tries to convince you. Think about what really makes your NAF tick. Try and have a "conversation" with it and find out what really scares it so much. You have to tell your NAF that you are in tune with its fears and understand that it's scared but that you're a big girl now and can take what comes. Your NAF must simply calm down and trust you! Now you can listen to all of your other voices – the positive ones. Set them free, and together you can silence that NAF!

Tip 3 – Compose instant mantras for calming your NAF

Now that you have identified your **Dominant NAFs,** it's time to compose mantras you can recite every time your NAF is on the attack. For best effect, repeat the mantra ten times consecutively. Its purpose is to remind you of something positive. Deep down, you believe that the message of the mantra is possible; but all is forgotten when your NAF goes into a tizzy!

Here are some examples:

If the "**Please Everybody NAF**" attacks you, you can say:
"I put myself first, and that's all right with me!"

Or if "**Kiddimus NAF**" is around, try:
"I am the best possible mother for my kids!"

For "**Controllus NAF**," try:
"I am letting go, and I feel calm."

For "**Failure NAF**":
"I am doing the right thing, and I will succeed!"

NAF:_____

Mantra: _____

NAF:_____

Mantra: _____

NAF:_____

Mantra: _____

P.S. Now that you've cracked Code No. 1- The Identification Code, don't forget to open the accompanying workbook to the first chapter and pamper yourself with some more "attractive" exercises!

CHAPTER 2

CRACKING CODE NO. 2 – FIND YOUR INNER CORE

"Let your heart guide you, it whispers, so listen closely."

— UNKNOWN SOURCE

> **So, what can we expect by cracking the second Code of the Law of Attraction – "Find Your Inner Core"?**
>
> We will learn about our "Inner Core," which represents the most important things in our lives: our passions, our loves, and our personal values. We will understand how discovering our Inner Core connects with our ability to become magnets that attract positive opportunities and a host of things we desire. We will examine to what extent our values feature in our lives and how our NAF influences them. We will learn what affects our decision-making processes and how we make important decisions. We will get tips and action steps on recognizing the things that are most important to us and learn how to focus on them.

The Find Your Inner Core code can be illustrated by the following conversation, which has remained etched in my memory since the day I heard it.

I was sitting with three women, one of whom proudly told the others that she would soon qualify as a certified meditation instructor. She told us of her dream to open a meditation center with a small natural food restaurant attached. Her "friends" immediately pounced on her, and shot her down. "That's crazy. There's so much work involved. It would be so stressful. You would never have any time to be with your kids."

The woman, who looked crestfallen, mumbled, "I guess so. It *would* be really difficult."

I couldn't help myself. I turned to the "friends" and asked, "Why are you killing her dream?"

One of the women answered bitterly, "Because that's life! I, myself, have a dream cemetery in my head."

A "dream cemetery?"

Let's not allow ourselves to become a cemetery for our dreams.

What is Your Inner Core?

Our NAF is very persuasive. It knows us inside-out and knows exactly which buttons to press to exert its influence. It never gives up. It attacks when we are most vulnerable (in the middle of the night, for example).

Careeristus NAF, for example, will convince us to stay in the same job and not to look for another, even if we are feeling unfulfilled, frustrated, and unhappy in our present position. It convinces us that we won't find a job with the same salary, conditions, and convenient working hours and location, and it tells us we're too old to make a change.

Our NAF convinces us, and we stay in the same job. So, why do we feel we're missing out on something? Why do we feel unhappy and frustrated? Why is there still something niggling deep inside us that won't go away, despite our NAF's powers of persuasion?

That "little something" is what prevents our NAF from completing its mission. That "little something" will not go away. That "little something" is our lifeline. Imagine the following:

Hiding deep down inside each of us is a precious pearl. Over the years the pearl has become caked with mud and dirt. With this heavy coating, the pearl no longer sparkles and shines. We are not even absolutely sure it's still there. But, if we clear a narrow path to the pearl, its light will start to shine inside us. It will influence our actions and allow us to clean away the layers of mud.

That "little something," the "precious pearl," represents the most important things in our lives, and if left unexpressed our pearl will be held captive by feelings of frustration, despair, worry, and missed opportunity. I call this "little something" the "Inner Core." Our Inner Core represents our true identity and what we really want, love, and yearn to do.

Our Inner Core has three main components:

- **Loves** – the people and things that we love in our lives.
- **Passions** – that fire that burns inside us for the things we must have (or must do) at any price.
- **Personal values** – the principles and loves that guide our lives naturally. Expressing these values will lead to personal satisfaction and self-fulfillment. Examples include creativity, independence, and volunteerism.

Why loves, passions, and personal values?

- Because those are the things that make us "who we are," a kind of internal mold that remains unchanged by external factors.
- Because if we are able to express those elements, we will feel a sense of satisfaction, inner peace, purpose and fulfillment.
- Because if we express what is within our Inner Core, we will radiate a positive feeling outward. This will do wonders for our ability to attract, and eventually so many opportunities will come our way that we will truly be more "attractive."

- Because these are the things most often neglected, pushed aside, and conceded under the pressures of every day life: obligations, commitments, and expectations.

- Because these are the things that we have to choose to include in our lives. For some reason, we push them aside in our daily routine, and we must make an effort to consciously change our habits and bring them into our lives, despite our fears and doubts.

This is probably just the time for a member of the NAF family to make its presence known and claim: "You don't have an 'Inner Core.'. You don't even know what you really love in your life, what you yearn for, and what your values are. You have no direction."

This is your chance to tell your NAF that everyone has an Inner Core, and that there is no person without loves, desires and values. The problem is that our Inner Core is quashed. In the hustle and bustle of daily life, we are so busy with our routine that we don't think about ourselves. In fact, we have completely forgotten what we really want and what is best for us.

The aim of this chapter is to help us understand why we quash our Inner Core, to teach us to recognize the components of our Inner Core, to focus on those things and to allow them a place of pride in our lives. If we focus on our Inner Core, we will be able to hear our other "internal voices," not just that negative voice through which our NAF speaks to us. Listening to those voices will eventually bring joy, satisfaction and tranquility, and it will enable us to attract what we want into our lives.

Tessa, one of my coachees, asked me, "What's wrong with me having grandiose dreams?"

"There's nothing wrong," I replied. "Why do you ask?"

"Because my friend says those dreams won't come true. I'd like to know if I really can attract them into my life."

"What are your dreams?" I asked.

"I want to win the lottery, or inherit a lot of money," she answered.

"So, you want someone to save you. You want to be passive and wait for good things to just fall your way," I interpreted.

"I beg your pardon?"

I told her that the Law of Attraction and dreams are relevant only for things that depend on us – events that we are able to influence. Our Inner Core, which is composed, essentially, of our dreams, becomes a reality only if we add to the equation the things that depend on us, not on some heavenly force. That is, indeed, the way to make Tessa's dreams, however grandiose, come true. It is the way to reshape her Inner Core so that it responds to her and becomes a part of her life. For example, if she wants to make a lot of money, there's nothing wrong with dreams like these:

"I want to open a chain of clothes stores, with branches all over the world".

"I want to be a famous writer, with novels that sell millions of copies".

Either of those dreams can really come true. Tessa can attract what she desires in life – if she is truly and wholeheartedly willing to do the work needed to realize her Inner Core, rather than merely sitting passively and praying for a winning lottery ticket.

Why is your "Inner Core" always pushed aside?

Have you ever thought about why we so love to be on vacation in far away places where we don't know anyone, can dress the way we like, and can do exactly what we want without being answerable to anyone? It's simple: nobody sees us, nobody hears us, and nobody knows us.

We are anonymous and detached from social pressures, criticism, and judgment.

One of the biggest influences on our NAF is our social environment. Our parents, siblings, friends, colleagues, and even the television constantly drum into us the things that are most important to them. They relentlessly remind us of their loves and their desires, their personal values, and the fact that what they think is right. But what about us?

We have absorbed the Inner Core of these other influences and sacrificed our own. Our very denial of our Inner Core causes negative thinking, which gradually takes over. Denying the things we love, the things we yearn for and want, enables a whole slew of NAFs to develop inside us, and slowly but surely to sidetrack us from realizing our Inner Core.

The more we distance ourselves from our Inner Core, the fainter the other voices (the positive voices) become, and the easier it is for the negative voices to overpower them. The further we distance ourselves from our Inner Core, the greater the intensity of the negative vibes we project into our environment. As a result, our ability to attract is impaired. Fewer and fewer good opportunities come our way. We become frustrated and the vicious cycle starts operating.

We can respect and appreciate the values, desires, and loves of the people around us, but first and foremost we must remember our own!

This process of distancing ourselves from our Inner Core is common to both men and women, but it is more widespread among women. The craving for communication and harmony among family members pushes us to concede. In order to avoid confrontation or to not feel that we are harming our partner's career, we put the things that we want on hold, in the belief that we can always carry on from where we left off... one day. As time goes by, our **Please Everybody NAF** becomes stronger and badgers us to "be there" for our children, for our partners, for our aging parents. The further we distance ourselves from our Inner Core the harder and more threatening the way back.

Nancy's Story

Nancy grew up in a large, poor family. Her father was a manual laborer who worked hard to provide for his family, while her mother kept house and took care of the children. As the years passed and the children grew up, they became carbon copies of their parents. Nancy's brothers turned to manual labor and provided for their families, while her sisters married and became mothers and full-time homemakers.

Nancy was always the exception. Even from an early age she had different priorities: studies, personal development, and economic independence. She wanted to succeed, to manage a large corporation, to build a glittering career and go far. After she graduated high school, Nancy worked as a waitress, saving every cent she earned to finance her studies. Her parents didn't understand her and complained that she was wasting her time, but Nancy knew that furthering her education was the only way to start to make her dreams come true.

After her university graduation, Nancy began to work as the product manager of a large corporation. She invested much of her time and energy studying and investing in personal development and enrichment. She knew she had to prove herself and to work twice as hard as anyone else if she wanted to excel in her field.

It was Nancy against the rest of the world: against her family who thought her relentless pursuit of a career was a hindrance to fulfilling her true purpose in life – to get married and raise a family; against her male colleagues, who began to notice the young female manager rising up through the ranks and competing with them for promotion; and against her company's senior management, to whom she constantly had to prove herself and her worth, while also retaining her femininity.

Give Up Now NAF reminded her that she was wasting her time, and that just being a woman in a man's world was her Achilles' heel. She would never be promoted if she was competing with a man…

Failure NAF kept drumming into her that the higher up the ladder she rose the pressure would only get worse and that it was better to quit while she was ahead…

Family NAF worked overtime to remind her of all the pain she was causing her family with her decision to choose a career over the "normal" life the women in her family were destined for.

But despite their pressure, Nancy did not allow the NAFs to control her life. She believed in her abilities as a manager, and in the values that she wanted to promote within the corporation. She slowly but surely advanced and fulfilled her ambitions and objectives. The law of attraction proved itself.

A few years later, Nancy was promoted to the position of Marketing Manager, and became General Manager following her company's merger with an international firm. Today, Nancy is the Vice-President of Marketing in one of the country's largest retail corporations, and is a loving mother to three children. She feels completely fulfilled in her professional life and enjoys new challenges and ventures.

Nancy was well aware of what her Inner Core contained. She radiated positive vibes and attracted the opportunities she'd been hoping for! Yes, it's true, Nancy managed to break through the glass ceiling and become one of the country's ten most successful businesswomen.

You can make it happen – if you really want to!

Why is it important to concentrate on your Inner Core?

Try and remember how you felt when you were in your prime – the best time in your life – when you were satisfied, contented, and fulfilled. Now try to remember some details about that period.

Do you remember how you seemed to blossom all over? Do you remember how good you felt and how much room there was in your heart for loving others? Do you remember how natural it felt to give of yourself, with no anger, resentment or envy? Do you remember how you were able to do everything, and how you were in control of your time?

And what about your ability to attract (even if you didn't know you had such ability)? Were you sending out positive vibes? Vibes of optimism and contentment? Do you remember how you managed to attract the things you wanted in life? How everything seemed to work out as you wanted it?

No, it's not a dream! That used to be our reality, a long time ago, and we can recreate this reality today if we implement the Inner Core principle.

Focusing on our Inner Core will allow us to silence our negative voices and introduce optimistic new voices of excitement, joy, and expectation into our lives.

Focusing on our Inner Core opens up many new unexpected opportunities, as illustrated by the following quotation:

> *"When you follow your heart, doors open in places that you didn't know existed, doors that would not open for anyone else but you." (Unknown source)*

If we pursue the things we love, surround ourselves with people we love, fulfill our desires, and live according to our true values, we will live our lives with such an amazing intensity that most of our NAFs will be sent winging their way straight back to NAFland. And we'll be attracting into our lives exactly what we want. In short, if we make our Inner Core a reality, we become "attractive" – a fact that has nothing to do with our outward appearance.

Gail's Story

Gail grew up in a family of lawyers. Her grandfather was a successful attorney, as was her father, and her brother followed suit, so to speak. It was taken for granted that Gail would follow in their footsteps and also become an attorney. From early on, it was obvious to her that she couldn't let her family down. There was no question but that Gail would study law. When she finished her internship as a criminal lawyer, Gail's father used one of his many connections to arrange a position for her in one of the country's foremost criminal law firms. Gail began to work night and day, at the expense of almost everything else in her life.

Though she knew that law was a full-time job, she never imagined how much extra time she would have to invest. Every hour a new problem arose, an extra task, yet another question, and Gail found herself drowning in the pressure of non-stop work. Her colleagues would compare the results of their cases, and Gail was afraid of coming up short. She was tormented by the competitive atmosphere of the office.

She had no time for herself, stopped meeting her friends, and hardly saw her husband. By the time she came home in the middle of the night, he was already asleep, and when they got up early in the morning to go to work, they barely had time to speak to each other. **Pressure NAF** and **Failure NAF** had a field day, planting all sorts of fears in Gail's head, tormenting her during the few hours she managed to sleep. In her dreams, Gail saw judges, attorneys, and angry clients. They were all shouting at her, telling her that she wasn't doing a good enough job.

She began to feel terribly tired during the day and found herself unable to concentrate. Yet, in spite of all that, **Please Everybody NAF** convinced her not to say *"No"* to the extra tasks that her bosses assigned to her. She found herself saying, *"Yes"* and slowly cracking under the severe pressure.

A couple of years later, Gail and her husband decided to start a family. She had no idea how she would manage to fit motherhood into her lifestyle, but she knew that she wanted a baby. Gail worked right up to her due date, without slackening her pace at all.

The turning point came during her maternity leave, after the birth of her first daughter. Gail suddenly discovered she was free. Ironically, even though she had a newborn baby to occupy her time, Gail suddenly found the peace and quiet she had been missing all her life.

Just for fun, she started to decorate the dresser she had bought for the new baby, and she became completely absorbed in the task. She tried out new colors and chose stencils, and was almost sorry when she finished the job. That's when she started decorating the stroller as well. Everywhere she turned there were things to paint and decorate – wooden toys, more furniture, and lots more. When her friends visited, they were amazed by her artistic handiwork and asked if she could decorate things for them, too. Gail was delighted to oblige, and this marked the beginning of her change of career.

Slowly but surely Gail became absorbed in the task of decorating, enjoying every minute of it. She was pleased with the end result, but, more importantly, felt satisfied and calm. Gail had made a change and realized her true potential. Instead of working under pressure in a threatening and competitive environment, she found an outlet for the personal values most important to her - creativity, independence, and serenity. Gail began to send out positive vibes of energy, enthusiasm, and contentment. And, as a result, the Law of Attraction began to bring her what she desired. Opportunities were not long in arriving. Orders for furniture and designs were flowing in, as were invitations to design shows. She was now working in a relaxed atmosphere, mistress of her own fate, knowing that she was doing the very best job she could. But even better, she suddenly had all the time and patience in the world to devote to her baby daughter.

Action Steps - A Moment With NAF

When you read about other women who succeeded because they managed to connect to the things they really love, and attract those things into their lives, your NAF is probably jumping up and down, shouting. So let's release it, once and for all.

Write down what your NAF is saying _____

_____

What are your other voices saying? _____

_____

_____

How to reveal your Inner Core:

In order to reveal our Inner Core we have to allow ourselves time to be alone, quietly, with no disturbances, to enable ourselves to reconnect with the things we have buried so deep down within ourselves.

To help you reconnect with the "important things in your life" I have prepared a list of questions, the answers to which will help you recognize the elements of your Inner Core.

The answers to these questions might not be immediately obvious, that's okay! Give yourselves a few days to think it over, think about your answers - do they really "feel" right? Do you feel a little shiver down your spine when go over them in your head? Is there anything else you want to add?

Action Steps- What do you really love?

(This exercise might not be easy, but if you take enough time to think about the questions the answers will start to flow.)

Who are the people you really love? The people that surround you, understand you, listen to you, share things with you, people who give of themselves and allow you to give of yourself?

What did you love to do in the past that made you feel good?

What did you love about your life in the past?

What do you love about your life now?

What do you do in your free time? What are your hobbies?

What do you like to do on weekends and vacations?

Have you ever received a prize? A certificate of commendation for excellence? If so, what did you do to earn it?

What about genetics? What did your mother/father/grand-mothers/grandfathers like to do, and what were their areas of expertise?

What are you passionate about?

The following story illustrates the essence of passion, and how our passions are buried deep inside us from an early age.

At one of my workshops, a mother told me about her eight-year old son and his "unrealistic" dream. His dream is to become a movie director. He spends all of his free time watching movies. His favorite subjects at school are drama and creative writing. He can reel off names of actors and movie directors and he'll tell you who won an Oscar and when. He is a walking movie encyclopedia. Yet, as she told me about her son, the mother didn't sound very enthusiastic about his choice of career.

I wondered what would happen to this boy's dream in the future. Where will he be in another twenty years? Maybe he'll outgrow his "grand passion," or maybe, when he gets older, his **Careeristus NAF** will tell him: "There is too much competition in the movie industry. Everyone fights over financing, and very few succeed. Choose something more practical." His **Failure NAF** might tell him: "You are not talented enough. You'll never make it." If, when the time comes, the boy chooses a career that doesn't allow him to express his Inner Core, he'll be disappointed. He'll probably feel he's missed out, not followed his heart, and not fulfilled his true dream – his passion. Passion is something that burns inside us and awakens inexplicable excitement. It is that spark of new ideas that wakes us up in the middle of the night.

Our passion opens the door to new opportunities and attracts into our lives what we most desire. On a popular radio program I heard recently, a famous singer was being interviewed about her new album. The host asked her what motivated her to constantly produce new albums and shows. Was it fear of failure that kept her creative mode working? The singer answered, "Not at all. My motivation is my burning passion to create, and to go on creating. It's the joy I feel when a new song is born and the satisfaction of performing it. It's that same passion that opens up new opportunities for me and lets me live my dream. There are lots of obstacles along the way, but I've learned to deal with them. The happiness I feel about fulfilling my passion outweighs everything else."

Action Steps – What Are You Passionate About?

Think of something you did in the past that made you feel... "Wow!" – incredibly satisfied.

What was it about that experience that made you feel so elated?

What things and experiences are you attracted to?

If you could do anything without the fear of failing, guaranteed to succeed, what would you do?

What are you curious to know more about? What things? What people?

What do you want so badly that you would be willing to do it for free?

If you had a million dollars, what would you do and how would you spend it?

For what would you be willing to pay any price to have in your life?

In which direction does your inner voice guide you?

For which "higher cause" do you feel committed to act?

What makes your heart beat? What makes you come alive?

What brings you joy? What excites you? What energizes you?

What's the Connection Between Your Strengths, your Loves, and Your Passions?

Another way of discovering our loves and passions is through our natural strengths and abilities. The more in tune we are with our strengths, the more we can rely on them. Our natural tendency is to focus on the areas in which we do not excel. We become angry, frustrated, and negative, totally ignoring our best qualities. But we're making a huge mistake there! There's a direct connection between our loves, our passions, and our strengths. And, naturally, there's a direct connection between our strong points and the Law of Attraction. If we manage to express our strong points in our lives, we'll emit positive vibes and energy. And in return, we'll attract what's really important to us!

Usually, we love what we're good at. We excel and advance in life by doing the things we're good at, and that is also the way to realize our potential. Therefore, it's essential to first identify our strong points and then to go about strengthening them! To strengthen what is strong, as crazy as that sounds. That's the way to satisfaction and self-fulfillment. So… if we sometimes find it difficult to locate our Inner Core, we should start with something familiar - our strong points, the things we're good at. That will bring us on a straight path to our Inner Core.

Action Steps- What are your personal values?

I invite you to join me on a "discovery tour" to identify your own personal values. (Our personal values are the third component of our Inner Core).

Stage 1: Here is a list of values. Check the ones that you feel are an important part of who you are - the values that must, simply must, be a part of your life.

My list of values:

Check the box next to each value that is important to you:

Personal Values	✔
To be creative, in any area	
To be independent	
To feel confident	
To be punctual, neat, and organized	
To be able to organize events, parties	
Beauty, elegance, aesthetics	
To grow, learn, advance	
To be adventurous, daring, try new experiences	
To speak or perform before an audience	
To lead, influence, command, manage	
To have fun, enjoy, play	
To be spiritual	
To teach, instruct, effect change in others	
To express myself orally	
To be fit, keep in shape	

Personal Values	✔
To be free	
To live simply	
To be outdoors, in nature	
To spend more time with myself, less with others	
To care for people	
To volunteer, help, contribute to others and to society	
To be in touch with people, connected to them	
To think, be interested and challenged	
To listen to what people have to say	
To cooperate, work as part of a team	
To care for wildlife, nature, and the environment	
To feel I belong, am part of a community	
Couple hood / family life	
What else?	
What else?	

Each value you selected will help you satisfy three "supreme values" in your life:

1. Fulfillment of your potential; self-realization
2. Inner peace and harmony
3. Balance

That is, if the values you marked are given expression in your life, those three supreme values will be expressed as well. And when those three values are expressed, you will be applying the Law of Attraction in a way that most enhances your life and makes you attractive! Note: You've probably noticed that several needs are missing:

To be respected and appreciated

To be loved

To impress

To be popular

To win

To be in control

To not be ignored

To be right, etc.

While we feel these qualities are essential to our lives, they are "needs" that are largely dependent on outside factors. They are determined by our environment. They are qualities we achieve only through other people; they are not our personal values.

Personal values, on the other hand, are already part of us and not dependent on the reactions of others. It can be important to you to help and contribute even if those around you show no appreciation; you may also be creative even when others do not approve.

Fulfilling our personal values brings us satisfaction and a sense of total personal fulfillment because we are doing something that comes from within us and is not connected to other people's actions or reactions. If we give our environment total control to dictate our needs, we're going to be constantly chasing our tails. While an unfulfilled need fills us with energy, it is negative energy that causes us pain and frustration. It seriously impairs what we project outward and, as a result, restricts our law of attraction and our ability to attract what we want.

Stage 2: Think about the best time in your life (the time when your NAFs were inactive or very quiet), when you were happy or experiencing a deep sense of satisfaction – an excellent indication that your values have found expression.

What made you feel happy at that time? What values were expressed? If you discover new values, add them to the list.

Stage 3: Think back to a stage when you felt frustrated. Which values were repressed and which expressed? Add these to the list.

Stage 4: Now that you have a list of values, what are you going to do with it? This is where the clarification process begins. Try and put aside the values that are less important to you and highlight only those that are deeply rooted within you. At first it might appear that these values are equally important, but in fact we all have a number of personal values that are the most essential values in our lives.

Go over all the values you listed and write down your five most important values here:

1 _____

2 _____

3 _____

4 _____

5 _____

Your Valuemeter

The Valuemeter is a tool I developed to clearly indicate our values and their level of expression in our lives:

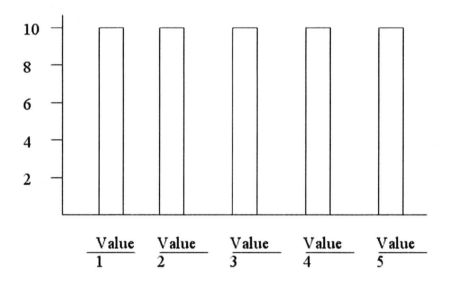

Action Steps – Prepare your Valuemeter

1. Note your top five personal values in the following graph:

2. Estimate the extent to which each of these values is expressed in your life, on a scale of 0-10 (with 0 meaning that the value is not expressed at all in your life and 10 meaning that it is fully expressed in your life). Color in the appropriate columns (using different colors or patterns for each value) to show how each value is expressed.

Here is an example of a Valuemeter:

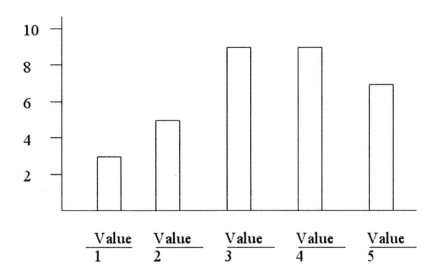

Value 1 - Influence = 3

Value 2 - Independence = 5

Value 3 - Aestheticism = 9

Value 4 - Organization = 9

Value 5 - Creativity = 7

From this example, we can see that the woman who filled in the Valuemeter feels that Aestheticism and Organization are well represented in her life, since they both scored 9. However, other values important to her, such as Influence and Independence, are represented to a lesser extent (scoring 3 and 5). It is hardly surprising that this woman feels frustrated professionally, since her hopes of being independent and influential have no expression in her life. Creativity, another important value, scored 7 – not a low score, but not high enough for her to be completely satisfied.

The Valuemeter served as a warning to this woman. She suddenly saw the true picture of her life and realized how it would continue if she didn't make a significant change.

Look at your own Valuemeter. What do you see? Which value is well represented in your life, and which is missing?

Focusing on your Inner Core means constantly striving to make your Valuemeter reach Maximum, so that your five most important values will have maximum expression (or close to it) in your life. Display your Valuemeter in a prominent place to constantly remind you of your Inner Core.

Every now and then you should review your Valuemeter. Repeat the exercise from the beginning and check whether your five most important values have remained the same and, if they are still expressed in your life to the same extent.

How can you attract more of what you want and less of what you don't want? Or, how can you better define your Inner Core?

It may be hard at this point to define exactly what's inside our Inner Core. We might not be able identify precisely what we want in life to achieve the satisfaction and inner peace we long for – the pleasure of getting up in the morning with a sparkle in our eyes and an overflow of energy.

The following exercise can sharpen the view of our Inner Core and therefore strengthen our ability to attract.

Action Steps – How Can You Attract More of What you Want?

If you are unable to define exactly what you want, love, and desire for your life you will continue to attract the things you don't want, and you'll keep doing so as long as you dwell on these things. Therefore you've got to start concentrating on what you do want. The following exercise helps you do just that:

1. Think of something that happens in your life, over and over again - and you let it happen even though you know it's not good for you.

   For example:

   You do poorly in job interviews. (Your Failure NAF is in control)

   You can't say "No." (Your Please Everybody NAF is in control)

   You can't manage to save money. (Your Money, Money, Money NAF is in control)

2. Make a list of all the undesirable behaviors you repeat again and again in your life. Note how you feel in each case.

3. Write the following question: "If I don't want this behavior to continue, what do I want to happen and how do I want to feel?"

4. Picture the perfect scenario in your mind, find the words that best express what you want, and write them down. That's the first step to repressing your NAFs and attracting your aspirations and your Inner Core into your life.

Why is it that discovering your Inner Core can make you feel uneasy – as if everything's a mess and you didn't really succeed at all?

Congratulations. You've discovered the components of your Inner Core, and, with great energy and enthusiasm, you've begun to fulfill everything inside. But all of a sudden, you feel tense, nervous, anxious. The ground seems to be shaking beneath you, and your old friends the NAFs are starting to raise their heads again…

Well, rest easy. That's a familiar and natural response. The simple explanation lies in the wide gap between the current state of our lives and the scenario we've defined for ourselves. The discrepancy between the vibes you're sending out right now (negative vibes resulting from dissatisfaction) and the vibes emanating from what you want and long for (positive vibes resulting from the Inner Core you've just defined) produces a period of change. Change causes tension and discomfort. We must understand that during transitions and times of change, when we are just beginning to learn what our Inner Core consists of, things may seem to be falling apart. We may even feel that we've failed or are headed in the wrong direction.

- If your goal is to attract an ideal type of client to your business, one that is not at all like your current clients, understanding this creates a state of dissonance. You send out negative vibes to your current clients and reflect back the vibes you gave off. The unfortunate result is that your current clients may leave you.

- If you aspire to a new career, one totally different from your current one, you've created dissonance. You send out negative vibes at your current place of work and reflect back the same. Your success and status in your current job take a downward turn.

The solution is to be aware and understand that the transition period between discovering your desires and fulfilling them may be disappointing, even disheartening. That's a natural and logical phenomenon, and we can overcome it as long as we rest assured that it will be replaced by fulfillment of our desires. Therefore, I advise setting priorities for the desires contained in our Inner Core. Rather than focus on all of our desires at once, we should work toward them one at a time.

Action Steps- When a Doubt Kills the Dream

Sometimes, we know what we want and long for, even dream about it at night, but our NAFs keep us from achieving it. They poke at our brains and inject strong doses of doubt and pessimism: "You're not worth it." "You don't deserve it." "Why do you have it coming to you?" "If you get it, something bad will result." These thoughts, inspired by your NAFs, send off negative vibes that prevent us from fulfilling our desires and attracting what we want.

The following exercise is one effective way of dealing with these NAFs:

Keep a notebook to mark down every time you want something and manage to achieve it, no matter how large or small a thing. These are times you acted consciously and attracted the desired results. You were hired for the job you wanted, you landed the man you were attracted to, you learned something new and interesting. The very fact that you proved yourself capable of doing these things, and attracting them into your life, is enough to convince you that any delay in getting what you want is temporary. Your dream will still come true if you keep believing and start acting as I've recommended.

NAF and Decision-making

Each new decision we make in our lives is a difficult process. But sometimes, as soon as we make that decision, we feel a sense of relief. We feel we've done the right thing. Although decisions are difficult, once we've made them it's easier to live with the consequences. This is not always the case if our decision-making process is influenced by one of our NAFs rather than by our Inner Core. If we consider our NAF and its needs during our decision-making process, we will never feel truly satisfied even if our NAF feels relief. We will always regret the results.

If we consider only our personal desires, if our decision is based on our Inner Core, we'll feel we did the right thing and be more confident about the results.

<u>Dinah's Story</u>

Dinah and Joe got married when they were 26. They were a good-looking and promising young couple, with an exciting future ahead. Joe had just completed his internship as a dentist, and Dinah was a newly qualified teacher. Dinah and Joe had always been inseparable, the perfect couple. That was how it appeared, at least. Hugs and kisses in public, pillow talk, and pet names.

Two years after their wedding day, their daughter Marla was born. Joe, the proud father, encouraged Dinah to give up her job and devote herself to their newborn daughter. Over the years, Dinah began to sense a change in Joe's attitude toward her. The more successful he became professionally and the greater his practice grew, the less interested he was in what was happening in her life. He wasn't involved in what went on at home, invested no time in their daughter, etc. Every time Dinah mentioned that she wanted to go back to work, Joe became angry and pressured her to stay at home, Just as his mother had stayed at home and dedicated her life to raising her children and keeping house.

The more affluent they became and the more luxuries they accumulated, the emptier Dinah's heart felt. She felt her marriage was falling apart, and she felt powerless to stop a snowball that was gaining speed by the minute. Her attempts to talk to Joe about their relationship, and maybe even seek counseling, were met with complete opposition.

She started thinking about the worst possible option – to split up with Joe. Dinah was obsessed by the struggle between the thought of separating from her husband or keeping the situation as it was – between living a life without love, with no gratification or self-esteem, or ending her marriage and breaking up the family. This was a perfect breeding ground for the NAFs to get to work: **"What Will they Say?" NAF** convinced her to continue leading everyone around her to believe that everything was normal. "Dinah and Joe, the perfect couple." None of their friends must ever know that there were cracks in the marriage.

Biological Clock NAF, whispered that Dinah had a next-to-nothing chance of finding anyone new at her age, and if she did, she'd probably be too old to have more children. And she'd had always wanted three, hadn't she?

Kiddimus NAF argued that their daughter would suffer badly from the breakup of the family, and so it would be better to stay together and avoid breaking her young and fragile heart.

Money, Money, Money NAF reminded her that her financial situation was very good now – Joe was making a good living. How did she think she'd be able to keep up such a high standard of living after a divorce, especially since she hadn't worked in the last few years and was out of touch with developments in her field. How did she think she'd be able to afford the designer clothes that now filled her closets? How would she be able to afford those skiing vacations abroad?

These thoughts tormented Dinah day and night, and each time she decided to gather her courage and do something, out popped one of the NAFs (which had been lying in wait) to convince her that she was about to make a terrible mistake. She could not involve anyone in her deliberations, since no one was allowed to know what really went on in her private life.

When Dinah heard about my workshops on the importance of living according to our values, she decided to do something.

Dinah filled in her Valuemeter. She discovered that love was her most important value, and that satisfaction and self-fulfillment were not far behind. But when she checked to see how these values were represented in her life, she realized that they did not feature at all. Dinah saw that in addition to living without her husband's love and appreciation, she had very low self esteem since she had no job and was not fulfilling her professional potential

Dinah understood that her NAFs were interfering with her life and her decision-making process. She realized that if she continued to listen to them she would stay miserable her whole life, project those vibes outward, and attract the things she doesn't want. If, on the other hand, she made a decision, however difficult it might be, to follow her heart, separate from her husband and begin the next stage of her life, there was a good chance she would be able to achieve the values most important to her and attract the components of her Inner Core.

Dinah gathered her courage and decided to make the break. She knew that their entire circle of friends would be in complete shock, but she also knew that those who might sever their contact with her were not her true friends in the first place. Dinah knew that in the past she had loved her job as a teacher and had always received warm and positive feedback from her pupils, who loved her. So she decided to go back to teaching, and to supplement her income by giving private lessons after school. Dinah knew that in the end the breakup of her marriage would have a positive effect on her daughter since she would finally be living with a mother who was fulfilled and calm.

Having made her final decision based on her Inner Core values, Dinah knew that she was strong enough to face the uncertainties of the future.

What's the connection between your NAF and the extent to which your personal values are expressed in your life?

Let's think about the connection between the dominant NAFs in our lives (those you identified in the first Code – The Identification Code), and the "minor" values on your Valuemeter.

Our decision-making process reflects this connection most clearly. When we make a decision, we hear many voices inside, all pulling us in different directions. The more significant the decision in our lives, the more prominent the connection becomes. If we listen carefully to these voices, we see that we can isolate the voice that expresses one or more of our major values, as well as the dominant voice, through which our NAF speaks to us.

When our major personal values have a low numerical representation on the Valuemeter, it indicates that decisions we made in the past were influenced by our NAF and not by our Inner Core.

There is another way our Valuemeter can help us in our decision-making process, particularly when we are faced with several conflicting values. One option might express one set of values, and another option a very different set of values, and it is difficult to decide. This is where the Valuemeter comes into play. As I've explained, it helps us to discover our most important Inner Core values. Once we become acquainted with these values we can make a decision that reinforces the most important ones, the ones with the highest Valuemeter readings. This does demand a sacrifice, since the other values are also important to us. But they are less important than our core values, and as long as these are the ones we follow we won't regret the decisions we make.

The Choice, and the decision, are yours alone

The decision to express our Inner Core values in our lives is not an easy one.

We might meet up with external opposition. Our "nearest and dearest" might try to convince us not to "take the risk" or to choose the path that they think is the right one for us. We will probably run into obstacles along the way that could lead to a stand-off with our NAF ("OK, so you tried it. Now do you see that it's not for you? There's no point in all this effort you're making. You might as well just give up now"). But in the long run, making sure that our Inner Core values are represented in our lives is the safest way to ensure a life of self-esteem and self-acceptance. The desire for an enjoyable and fulfilling life is stronger than anything else.

Just one more small thing...

This next section is meant for those women who did all the exercises but still haven't discovered your Inner Core. You must be thinking, "I've got no passions. I've got no inner core! I have no idea what it is I truly desire, what will bring the sparkle back into my eyes, what will make me feel energized and motivated and... Just feel good."

Let me reassure you – there's no need to worry. We all have an Inner Core, Values, loves, and passions. It just occasionally takes a bit of time to recognize them. With the tools you received in the previous chapter, you'll be able to identify the right opportunities for you when they arrive. When it happens, you won't miss it. You'll catch those opportunities with both hands, and you'll be absolutely sure of it! You'll know you've found your Inner Core.

No one is without an Inner Core. We all have one. You, too! You may need a little patience, but if you want to find it, you surely will.

And now, as promised, my tips for Code No. 2 – Find Your Inner Core

Tip 1 - Listen to your other voices

Over the course of a week, start to listen to all the other voices (those positive ones) that you've ignored until now. What did you enjoy doing in the past? What do you enjoy doing now?

Prepare a list of five things you enjoy doing and that you are able to do without excessive effort. Try and integrate them into your life, even daily. You can start small. Do it just for fun. It doesn't have to be a complicated "production."

There might be voices telling you: "You haven't got time, you don't have the money. What benefit will you get from an art class once a week?" Ignore those voices and do it anyway. You'll discover the reason when you read Chapter Six - Spring Into Action.

Tip 2 – Discover your Strengths

Being able to recognize our natural talents helps us to find our Inner Core. We usually most enjoy doing the things we are good at. Sometimes we're unaware of our natural talents. Outsiders (people close to us and people we trust) can teach us a lot about ourselves.

Talk to three different people, and ask them:

1. What are my most prominent abilities/strengths?
2. When are these qualities most evident?
3. If I were featured on a magazine cover, which magazine would it be, and what would the article be about?

Tip 3 – Discover your Partner's Inner Core

Try to think, on your own at first, what might be in your partner's Inner Core. What things are most important to him? What does he enjoy doing? What are his passions, and what are his personal values?

Discuss your findings with him, and check how well you really know your partner's Inner Core.

Think together about whether the important elements of his Inner Core feature in his life, and about what you can do to increase their presence.

P.S. Now that you've cracked Code No. 2 - Find Your Inner Core, don't forget to open the accompanying workbook to the second chapter and pamper yourself with some more "attractive" exercises!

CHAPTER 3

CRACKING CODE NO. 3 – THE POWER OF THOUGHT

"Human beings, by changing the inner attitudes of their minds, can change the outer aspects of their lives."

—WILLIAM JAMES

So, what can we expect by cracking the third Code of the Law of Attraction – "The Power of Thought"?

We will see who controls whom, whether we control our thoughts or our thoughts control us. We will understand the immense latent power of our thoughts. We will learn how to channel our thinking from our NAFs to a more quiet and peaceful direction. We will discover, and practice, a thinking process that creates a positive reality – "enabling thoughts." We will identify "stifling thoughts" and learn how they affect our ability to attract. And we'll get tips and action steps on how to focus on and control the power of thought.

Who Controls Whom? Do we control our thoughts or do they control us?

How many times do we find ourselves repeating the same basic task again and again, just because, with other things on our minds, we don't concentrate as we should?

How many times do we feel mentally exhausted because we constantly fret over the problems of daily life?

How many times do we pray silently for just a bit of mental peace and quiet?

Enough! We are sick and tired of thinking so much!

The NAF syndrome buzzes round our heads and allows us no respite. When we spend hours upon hours at work, **Careeristus NAF** whispers, *"You are not good enough, and your boss doesn't appreciate you. Spend even more time at work. Show him how conscientious you are."* In another corner we have **Kiddimus NAF** reminding us that *"You're neglecting your children. Why did you bother having them in the first place? So your babysitter could raise them?"* And then, when we get home and our children want our attention and ask us to play a game with them, our **Pressure NAF** reminds us that *"You don't have time to mess around playing games now. You have too much work to do."*

If we decide to entertain guests, **"What Will They Say?"** NAF jumps up and tells us that *"Ruth will be offended if you don't invite her. Call her now."* We do so, and then **Please Everybody NAF** butts in and reminds us that *"You know that Susan won't come if Ruth is there. They can't stand the sight of each other."* We are tortured by our NAFs, but continue to legitimize it by fuelling it with information. This routine drains all our positive energy, which could have been channeled in another direction, and we are left exhausted, with no desire to do anything – completely drained of energy.

Imagine yourself doing a chore you hate, such as washing dishes. Now imagine yourself washing dishes all day, every hour of every day, every day of the month, glass after glass, plate after plate. You're feeling stressed, you're suffering, but you continue to wash those dishes. You have no time for your family, no time for the activities and hobbies you love. You are trapped doing this one horrible job, with no chance of a reprieve.

Sounds awful, doesn't it?

That is what we do to our brains when we subject them to our NAFs. Our brains end up working overtime, concentrating mainly on things that are bad for us. We become weaker and lose our ability to stand up for ourselves. Our NAFs seize the opportunity and become stronger, eventually taking control of our thoughts.

How long? How long will we allow our thoughts to control us? How long will our NAFs be in charge of our lives? The time has come to put a stop to this, and it is possible. We can take control of our thoughts. We can focus on the power of thought and achieve results.

What are "Enabling Thoughts" or "Reality-creating" Thinking?

Have you ever heard of people who always get sick on their vacations? Or people who lead their lives just fine until some sudden event stops them in their tracks? Perhaps you've heard this statement: "I don't know why I keep attracting the wrong men, the ones who are no good for me."

And now, for the million dollar question: Do these things happen by chance? Or was it something these people were thinking about that attracted these events into their lives? Sorry to disappoint you, but I have no intention or pretense of imparting knowledge about mind-reading or the occult. However, I will say that our thoughts are composed of a type of energy that affects our environment and attract things into our lives.

According to the Law of Attraction, we attract the things we think about. Our thoughts create our reality, and they create opportunities. Imagine yourself successful, work toward this goal, and you *will* succeed. Imagine yourself surrounded by true friends, and you'll discover them. Imagine yourself failing, and – sorry to say – that is what's likely to happen.

As José Luis Sampedro wrote in his book, *The Etruscan Smile*, "You heard me right, my boy. What difference does it make if my mouth is closed? When you think with your soul, they hear you! Learn: Look at someone very, very closely and think. Just mutter, 'I'm going to butcher you,' and the person will collapse, I'm telling you… It's the same with good wishes: You see a woman and imagine her in your bed, and she's already half-way in your pocket… You know, I thought about my sheep, where I would bring them next day, and they nearly got there themselves… Even animals take note!"

For better or for worse, whether we want to or not, we attract into our lives what we concentrate on and invest our energy in! Nothing happens by chance.

Statements such as, "It's fate" or "The world is teaching me a lesson" are off the mark. If the same thing keeps popping into our lives over and over, it's not fate or destiny at work. It's a sign that we were concentrating on it, sending out certain vibes that brought results. We attracted the very same things into our lives in return, and they shaped our current reality. Therefore, when we repeat the same habits, good ones or bad, our mode of thinking – which we ourselves created - is determining our reality.

What we must now do is check to see that the reality we created for ourselves is, indeed, the reality we desire – the best reality we can hope for - and not the one that was the inevitable result of negative thinking. In other words, we need to create a situation in which we control our own thoughts – and our thoughts do not control us.

The Choice is Yours

Picture your thoughts as a muscle. Until now, you've been exercising that muscle in a certain way, which produced a particular reality. Now, if we want to change our pattern of thinking to create a different reality, we've got to begin training that muscle to work differently. We have the power to train and control our thoughts. We can focus on our power of thinking and achieve results!

In nearly every aspect of our lives we have the right to choose. Just as we can choose where to live, we can choose who we want to associate with and befriend, which school to send our children to, and, most importantly, what we think!

The key lies in this one simple but important fact: We can only think about one thing at a time. **We cannot concentrate our thoughts on two things simultaneously.**

Does that sound strange? Try this simple exercise:

Action Steps – Focusing

For the next minute, focus your thoughts on your son - how you sent him off to school today, what he was wearing, what he ate for breakfast, etc. (You can, of course, focus on any other subject that comes to mind.)

Now check whether you thought about anything else during that minute.

If so, you allowed another thought to sneak in, and it came at the expense of - not simultaneously with - the original thought.

Try again and again, until you feel that you have successfully focused on all the little details of your chosen subject for a whole minute.

Remember, I am not claiming that from now on we'll refrain from thinking any negative thoughts at all. I'm merely demonstrating that we can control how many negative and positive thoughts we think as a result, the outcome we desire is within our control. It all depends on the choices we make.

When Sharon came to my workshop she was filled with dread. She told me that her husband was due to travel to Europe for a conference and that she would be staying behind at home with their two children. She didn't know how she'd cope. Her husband is a full-time father. He always helps. He's always around and always cooperates. Without him, even for one week, Sharon couldn't imagine how she'd manage to juggle everything – her work, her studies, caring for the children – with no support system to rely on. Everything fell on her shoulders! How would she cope?

I told Sharon about the immense power of thought and explained to her that the choice was hers. She (and only she) could channel her thoughts in the direction she wanted. She could remain scared and miserable, or she could choose to see the positive side of her husband's trip. Sharon decided to put this technique into practice and began to think about all the positive things that would result from her husband's trip to Europe. She started by thinking about the professional success her husband would reap from his trip, and then she thought about all the little things she could do while her husband was away, such as hosting a "girls party" or watching television until the wee hours of the morning. Each time **"I Can't Do It On My Own" NAF** reared its ugly head, Sharon focused her thoughts on the positive aspects of the trip and on all the fun things that she could do by herself.

In the end, Sharon discovered that she couldn't wait for her husband to actually leave on his trip.

Apart from its latent power in channeling our thoughts to see the glass half-full rather than half-empty, positive thinking can also influence the way others perceive us:

The magazine ***Marie Claire*** conducted an interesting study to prove the power of positive thinking. They chose Nicole, an ordinary woman who wears size-44 clothes, and plastered her picture on enormous posters. They divided the posters into two sets, each with a different caption under the identical picture.

Half the posters bore the caption:

"I think I'm fat. What do you think?"

While the other half we're entitled:

"I think I'm sexy. What do you think?"

Marie Claire then surveyed thousands of people and asked them what they thought about Nicole – was she fat, or was she sexy? What do you think most of them thought about Nicole?

Yes, you got it. It seems that most people agreed with what Nicole thought about herself. When she declared herself to be fat, 55% agreed with her, and when she called herself sexy, amazingly enough, 66% agreed with her.

Does that sound strange? Not at all! The way people feel about us depends largely on the way we perceive ourselves and what image we portray to those around us. There is no "proven fact" that our NAF can wave in our faces, because at the end of the day other people's reactions to us are a direct result of how much we fuel our NAF.

Well, so what do you say? Sexy or fat? The bottom line is that it all begins and ends in our heads.

And now, now that we understand that the choice lies in our hands, and that we have the right and the power to decide what to think about, when to think it, and how to present ourselves to other people, and we remember that we can only think about one thing at a time, we can practice focusing on the power of thought.

So, how do we do it?

Shine the beam of light in the direction you want

Imagine yourselves in a dark room, with a flashlight in your hand. When you shine the flashlight in a certain direction, you can see only the things illuminated by the shaft of light.

Now, compare shining that flashlight with focusing your power of thought. Just as you can change the direction of the light, you can shine the beam away from your NAF and the negative thoughts filling your brain, and toward your Inner Core, which contains all that makes you feel good, cheerful, and satisfied.

Each time your NAF tries to grab the flashlight to shine the beam of light in its direction, you must tighten your grip and keep the beam shining in the direction of what you want to illuminate, toward the reality you want to attract.

In one of my workshops, a teacher told me that she had learned an important lesson from the mother of one of her students. She told me that on the day of the parent-teacher conference, a happy, smiling mother entered her classroom. The teacher was slightly confused, as this was the mother of one of the worst students in class, one who never managed to improve her grades.

The mother made herself comfortable, and said: "I know exactly what you're going to tell me about my daughter. I know that her grades aren't good, and that she's one of the weakest students in class. But I want to tell you one or two things about my daughter that you don't know. My daughter is a wonderful child. She loves to draw and spends every day doing something artistic. Her pictures adorn every wall in our house. My daughter knows what she's good at, and we value that. We try to strengthen her talents. So what if she doesn't excel in her studies? Does that mean she's worth less as a person? My husband and I decided we wouldn't allow this parent-teacher conference to spoil anything. She's trying to improve, to understand and to study, and she studies a few times a week with a private tutor. But there's no way in the world that I'll allow her academic weaknesses to detract from her self-confidence. I love my daughter the way she is, and I know she'll go far, even without straight A's in math."

The teacher looked at the mother with admiration and thanked her sincerely for teaching her an important lesson in parenting.

That mother could have succumbed to the pressures of **Kiddimus NAF**, who would claim that *"Your daughter is not clever. She is the weakest student in the class. You don't do enough to help your daughter improve her grades. What kind of a mother are you? How can you show your face at the parent-teacher conference?"* But she chose to direct the beam of light in the positive direction: *"I know who my daughter is, I know what she's worth, and I'm strengthening her talents - the things she's good at and enjoys."*

The mother was aware of her daughter's academic standing and provided her with the help she needed. But she did not allow the situation to control her; she controlled the situation. In terms of her ability to attract, the reality she attracted was one of mutual respect. She created a supportive relationship between herself and her daughter. Most importantly, she inspired self-confidence in her daughter, the sense that she herself was worth something even if her grades were not skyrocketing. So, every time one of those annoying NAFs tries to grab your flashlight, remind yourself to shine the beam in a different direction, a better direction. Since you can already recognize the components of your Inner Core, you can fill your thoughts with them and illuminate them with your beam of light.

Judy's Story

Judy loved to paint. And she took to it like a fish to water. She liked the feel of dipping her brush into the richly colored oil paints and spreading them across the canvas. When she painted, she felt she was truly alive, not just existing. Despite her passion for painting, she never managed to gather her courage and fulfill her greatest dream – to mount an exhibition to gain public attention and sell some of her many works. Judy's paintings, apart from the ones hanging in her home and her husband's office (where she worked at the reception desk), were stacked in a closet, out of sight. Every time clients entered the office, they would glance at her fabulous paintings and pour on the compliments. But Judy ignored them. **Worthless NAF** told her they were just being polite, that her paintings were worthless. **Failure NAF** convinced her that even if she mounted an exhibition, no one would show up and even if they did they wouldn't stoop to actually buying a picture. **"What Will They Say?" NAF** retorted by saying that she'd be embarrassing herself by displaying her work publicly, and she'd become known as "the artist who never sold a painting." So, the years passed, and Judy grew increasingly frustrated. The negative vibes she was projecting paralleled her overwhelming sense of failure, and, indeed, she attracted exactly the thing she was focusing on – no recognition for her artwork and no realization of her dream.

She came to me for advice when she felt she could no longer

cope with the situation. I explained the principle behind our ability to attract the things we long for into our lives. I told her she could practice thinking thoughts that painted a positive reality. She could shine her flashlight in a different direction - away from her NAFs and toward her dream.

First, I asked Judy to define her dream in precise terms. She described the exhibition she had in mind - the paintings she chose to hang, the prices she planned to ask for them, what she would wear, how she would design the invitation, who she would invite, what speech she would give, what refreshments she would serve, and, most important, what an enormous success the event would be. As she spoke, Judy's eyes began to sparkle. Enthusiasm and positive energy were flowing through her. She was clearly ready for the next step.

I warned Judy that at the same time she was illuminating the positive, she'd need to cope with the NAFs that were still prancing around in her mind. She had, indeed, rejected any compliment she ever received on her artwork, thinking that people were trying to be polite but speaking empty words. I asked Judy to pay close attention each time one of her husband's clients compliments her paintings and to write down exactly what was said. She was to thank the speakers and later go back and read - slowly and carefully - everything she'd written. She did just that and was surprised at how quickly her notebook filled with an array of compliments that arrived almost quicker than she could record them. She read each one several times, and, despite herself, began to smile and actually believe what she was reading.

The third step was to ask Judy to take her paintings out of her closets and drawers and show them to people, letting them know at the same time that she was interested in mounting an exhibition. She followed through and did just that, and the outcome she was hoping for was just around the corner. One morning, a neighbor came to visit and Judy showed her some of her paintings. The neighbor mentioned that one of her best friends was an art dealer and might be interested in Judy's work. She invited her friend over to Judy's house, and after viewing several of the paintings the dealer said something Judy will never forget: "Your paintings are wonderful, and I'd be happy to exhibit them at my gallery. You just keep on painting, and I'll worry about all the rest."

You can imagine what Judy felt in her heart. Just be sure to draw the right conclusion: Judy moved her flashlight from her NAFs to her Inner Core and began focusing on what was good for her – the things she desired and wanted to attract into her life. She stuck with it and reaped the benefits. Judy had a highly successful solo art exhibition!

How do you practice thinking enabling thoughts that attract a positive reality?

Focusing on the power of thought, to enable yourself to direct the beam of light in the direction you want and attract a positive reality, requires a lot of practice.

Will our lives change when we change our thoughts? Yes, with the following caveat…

If we have 50,000 thoughts per day, and of those, 45,000 are negative, we will experience no difference. We'll continue to attract what we don't want into our lives. But if we practice in a disciplined manner over time, it will work!

Your NAF, of course, will try with all its might to oppose you, saying that what you're doing is childish and stupid, that it's not you. But if you persevere and continue thinking "enabling thoughts" that create your desired reality, you'll be amazed to discover how effective the method is. With time, your NAF will calm down and you'll feel more comfortable with the images you're projecting in your mind. You'll be on your way to changing the reality of your life.

Here are several techniques that were useful to women who practiced the art of thinking enabling thoughts in my workshops:

- Project positive images within your mind.
- Enter your Zen – Focus on an activity in which you are now engaged.
- Live the moment – The present is a present.
- Use all your senses.
- View the cup as half-full, even when the going gets tough.

- Prevention is better than cure.
- Knock on wood - ward off the evil eye.

1. Project a "Positive Mental Scenario" Within Your Mind

This is the first technique to practice thinking enabling thoughts that attract a positive reality.

We must realize that we are the lead players and the directors of our own movies.

When we imagine ourselves doing or performing something, our brain cells emit waves that transmit a message saying, essentially, that we have actually completed the task. When we transmit a message of success to our subconscious, and we project the scenario we have in mind, we've already traveled a good part of the road to success.

Action Steps- Project the Mental Scenario You Want

Let's say you have a fear of public speaking. Every time you address an audience, you start sweating and shaking. When this happens, you need to imagine a film in which you are standing before an audience, lecturing eloquently and calmly, in total control and with no fear whatsoever. Your audience is pleased and aroused by your presentation, and there are many questions for you at the end. The more detail you add to this positive scene, the clearer it will become in your mind and the more amazed you'll be at the results that will soon follow. This is your chance to step into the shoes of one of Hollywood's greatest directors and produce, direct, and star in a mental scenario that you desire and that will create a positive reality in your life.

Again – we must focus on what we want in life, not on what we don't want. I'm sure we all remember when, as kids playing catch, we saw the ball coming toward us suddenly and said to ourselves, "Please, just don't let me drop it. If I do, everyone's going to laugh at me." And what happened? We dropped the ball, of course. Why? When we project a negative experience at ourselves, dropping the ball in this case, we'll see a picture of ourselves experiencing exactly what we projected.

The conclusion? We must never tell ourselves what not to do. Rather, we must imagine a scenario in which what we want to happen actually happens. The brain functions on pictures. Our subconscious needs pictures to let it know what we want to attract into our lives. After getting the pictures, our sub-conscious updates the brain, telling it how to operate. Our thinking process uses the brain in the only way it knows how – by creating pictures. If our mental scenarios and thoughts project, for example, "I don't want to fail in my job interview," then our brains will receive a picture of failure. During the job interview itself, rather than projecting a "Don't screw up here" scenario, create one that says, "I'm calm, and I'm going to succeed." In this way, the scenario you project to your brain will be composed of pictures of success. And success won't be long in coming.

2. Enter your Zen- Focus on the task at hand

This is the second technique to practice thinking enabling thoughts that attract a positive reality.

The power of thought works like one of our body organs. Sometimes, if the organ is seldom used, we need to exercise it and use it to see results. Just like a swimmer who does daily laps, a runner who visits the track no matter what the weather, and a musician who practices diligently, we have to train ourselves to focus our power of thought on the things we want.

Our tendency to think negative thoughts and provide fodder for our NAF began a long time ago, and daily practicing has only served to make us better at it. The tendency has become second nature to us – a habit that's hard to break.

In the same way, if we train our thoughts to focus on the positive, and practice over and over again, positive thinking will eventually become a habit and will calm our NAFs.

Imagine the following scenario: Your partner is on the telephone talking to a colleague, and you're trying to tell him something important at the same time. Does your partner react? There's a prize for anyone who can truthfully say that her partner notices her and pays her any attention at all during his telephone conversation.

Does that situation sound familiar? Unlike women, men concentrate only on the task at hand. We women are the "multitaskers" who can do any number of things simultaneously and be aware of the details of each one.

I'd like you to "try on" this male attribute. Think about what would happen if you concentrated only on the task at hand. I promise you that only good will come of it!

When was the last time you made any progress on something you were engaged in and devoting your full energies to, without thinking about anything else? When was the last time you concentrated totally on what you were doing "here and now," without being diverted by worries about other matters? In other words, when did you last enter your own Zen and simply go with the flow, without making other plans or burying yourself in worries?

Was it at your last trip to the beach?

Was it when you were working in the garden?

Perhaps while you were watching a great movie?

Or maybe you don't remember at all when it was because it's been so long since you entered your ZEN.

Concentrating on the task at hand pushes our NAFs aside. We don't have time to fret and think negative thoughts.

If your children ask you to play with them right now, go ahead and play with them, wholeheartedly. Don't think about anything but the game itself, the rules, what is happening, and, of course, how much you're enjoying yourself with your children. The **Pressure NAF** will try and butt in to remind you that *"You have a whole pile of washing waiting to be folded"* or *"You haven't sent the email to that client yet"* or *"You have to call Fred urgently. Do you think playing is all you've got to do?"* Just ignore those negative thoughts and get on with the game.

In the same way, try to concentrate on every activity you undertake during the day, whether it involves work, home, or friends.

If we try to think about the last time we really enjoyed ourselves and attracted the positive reality we wanted, it was most likely a time when we immersed ourselves 100 percent in what was happening and focused on the task at hand – not on the outcome.

When was the last time you let go with a real belly laugh? When did you last watch a good movie or read a fascinating book? On these occasions, you concentrated completely on the task at hand without allowing any of your NAFs the tiniest crack to worm its way in. These were times you wholeheartedly enjoyed yourself. Why shouldn't you try to recreate these moments again and again and integrate them into your daily routine?

<u>Tracey's Story</u>

Tracey was a talented young lady with a successful career. In her job as department manager in a large factory, she met many people, held staff meetings, participated in management meetings, and met with clients. Her schedule was always very busy.

Despite her career success,. Tracey was unable to overcome one problem that had bothered her ever since she was young. She knew it was a common problem that affected many people, but that was no comfort. Tracey suffered from sweaty palms. Every time she had to shake hands with someone, her palms began to sweat and she prayed that the person facing her wouldn't notice. Tracey tried everything possible to avoid shaking hands. She didn't want anyone to discover her problem and was prepared to do anything to hide it. Before every important meeting, she paced the floor thinking about the best way to avoid shaking hands when she entered the room.

Finally Tracey decided on a new tactic. Luckily it was winter, and she decided she would wear gloves to avoid the problem, since no one would notice that her hands were sweating. And so,. Tracey started to wear gloves to her meetings and didn't hesitate to shake hands. After the handshake, when she removed her gloves, she was amazed to find that her hands had remained dry. Suddenly Tracey realized what this actually meant. Wearing gloves freed her from the stress of the handshake. With the help of the gloves,. Tracey was able to stop concentrating on the handshake itself and on how the other person would react to the feel of a sweaty palm. As long as she focused on the person facing her at the moment, and the conversation they were having, her hand remained dry. Tracey decided to adopt the trick of focusing on the main event, and not on what was worrying her and making her feel wretched.

At her next meeting,. Tracey plucked up her courage and left her gloves behind. Of course, you can guess what happened. Her hands remained dry and she was able to smile throughout the entire meeting. At the end of the meeting she felt brave enough to try another "farewell" handshake, and, amazingly enough, her hand stayed dry.

That is the power of our thought.

3. Live the moment – The present is a present

"Today is the tomorrow we worried about yesterday." (Unknown Source).

The third way to create a positive reality for ourselves is to live the present, the here and now.

Everyone in the world is granted the same amount of time per day, no more or less than 24 hours. The difference lies in how each of us makes use of that time.

There's a movement in Europe called "Slow Food." Its symbol is a snail, and its purpose is to convince people to eat and drink slowly, to take the time to enjoy the flavors, to relish the preparation and quality of our meals. The movement opposes the concept of fast food and the lifestyle it represents. What's surprising is that Slow Food has become the basis for a wider movement called "Slow Europe," which was featured in the magazine Business Week. Many people live their lives in a race against the clock, and by the time they catch up it's too late.

There are people so anxious to live the future that they forget there's a present, the only time that truly exists. We must learn to take advantage of every moment to create a positive reality for ourselves! To paraphrase John Lennon: *"Life is what's happening now, while we're planning for the future."*

4. Use all your senses

When was the last time you knowingly used all five of your senses to experience something? The fourth technique to practice thinking enabling thoughts that attract a positive reality, is to use each one of your senses.

We were blessed with five senses for a reason. Undoubtedly, each one has a distinct function in our lives, but they also have additional functions that I'd like to reveal to you right now

As I've said, focusing on the power of thought, or controlling our beam of light, comes as a result of practice and training. One way to practice is to use each and every one of our senses. If we concentrate on what we feel right now, we will silence our NAF and prevent it from taking root. One excellent way to activate all five senses is to take a nature walk.

Try and make time for a daily walk. As well as improving your physical fitness and shaping your figure, a daily walk will relax you. As you start your walk, decide that for the next ten minutes you will concentrate solely on your sense of sight. In other words, examine the leaves on the trees and the colors, check out the houses en route, enjoy the gardens you pass, look at the children in the playground, etc. After that, for the next ten minutes, concentrate solely on your sense of smell. Which scents fill the air? Do you notice the scent of the first rain? Can you sense that your neighbor just pulled a fresh cake from the oven? Do you smell the blossoms on the trees? The exhaust from the cars?

And so it continues: For the next ten minutes, concentrate solely on your sense of hearing. What do you hear? The crackle of dry leaves? A baby crying? Children playing? Background music or a program on television?

As you continue on your walk, you'll realize that you're using senses you don't normally use in this kind of situation. Unlike children, who see everything and notice every little detail, we adults, unfortunately, stopped noticing such "trivialities" long ago. We carry the burden of the world on our shoulders and are trapped in the frenzy of our NAFs, which prevents us from enjoying the small things in life, such as flowers growing at the roadside.

5 View the cup as half-full, even when the going gets tough

The half-full cup: This is the fifth technique to practice thinking enabling thoughts that attract a positive reality. Our lives don't always reflect what is actually happening to us; they reflect the way we view what is happening. Our daily challenge is to turn a problematic situation into an opportunity. If we believe, as I mentioned, that nothing can go right in our lives, that is precisely what will happen! If we continue to concentrate on what is bad, the only things we'll attract are those we want to avoid. Whenever we go to battle with life, life always wins. But if we can find even a small crack through which we can project something positive, shine a ray of light and focus on it, it will be the start of attracting a new, positive reality, even at the most difficult times.

Diane's Story

Diane had been working for seven years as a systems manager at the same firm. She is a shy and quiet woman and an efficient, professional, and trustworthy employee. Her problems began when she got a new boss. He was new to the firm and intent on proving to everyone how important, powerful, and decisive he was. Diane, with her reserved nature, didn't get along with him. He was blind to her contribution to the firm and never gave her the chance to demonstrate it. He changed her job title and duties. Diane began to hate the firm, a place she only a short time earlier considered a second home. Getting ready to go to work each morning was torture. At night her NAFs were having a ball: **Worthless NAF** told her she had no talent, none that her boss would ever recognize, anyway. **"What Have I Done To Deserve This?" NAF** whispered messages of self-pity, complaint, and perpetual victimhood. **Failure NAF** drilled into her head that she'd never find another job and that even if she did she wouldn't be hired. If, by some miracle, she landed another position, nothing would change. She'd continue to suffer no matter where she worked.

As Diane's NAFs went to work on her, she began sending out negative vibes to her environment. Those vibes only served to attract more dissatisfaction, both from her new boss and from the jobs she'd begun interviewing for but not getting.

By the time Diane came to me for training, she was totally disappointed and discouraged. She lacked the energy to make the necessary changes and had no faith that any new job would be better than her current one.

I explained to Diane that she had the ability to attract and that the reality of her life lay in her hands. She could use the Law of Attraction to achieve the situation she desired and could focus her thinking to create a new reality. We analyzed her current situation and saw that she was afraid any new job would be identical to her last one. In other words, she was afraid of attracting what she did not at all want. It seemed that Diane was inside a vicious cycle. As long as she kept concentrating solely on the negative aspects of her job, she was attracting only similar types of jobs as alternatives and missing out on opportunities for much more satisfying positions.

I told Diane that the best way of escaping the cycle she'd entered would be to focus on whatever positive aspects she could find in her negative situation. We began to analyze her current job and try to come up with something positive about it, even though it was clear that she wanted to leave. We considered her salary, her colleagues, the location…

Diane saw one ray of light in a project she was working on that had no connection with her boss. She described the project for me – what it entailed, how she felt working on it, what she loved about it – and eventually she left the loop and stopped projecting negative vibes in every direction. She started emitting positive energy and began perceiving the cup as half-full rather than half-empty. With that and a bit of patience, she was hired for a new job, one that answered all her (positive) expectations. Diane understood that if she didn't change her pattern of thinking about her current job and find something positive to focus on, she would have the ability to attract – but she would only be attracting things she didn't want. By focusing on the half-full cup, Diane began attracting what she truly wanted.

6. Prevention is Better than Cure

This is the sixth technique to practice thinking enabling thoughts that attract a positive reality. Try to think of situations in which you are swept into the frenzy of your NAFs. Track these incidents in your mind, and try to stop them before they happen.

Many women experience NAF frenzy just before they fall asleep or when they wake up in the middle of the night. At night, when everyone else is snoring, we often find ourselves tossing and turning, unable to fall asleep and allow our brains to rest.

Failure NAF and **Pressure NAF** remind you that the important presentation you have to give tomorrow morning will be a total flop because you didn't fully prepare it.

Malignant NAF pops up and reminds you to start worrying about your check-up at the doctor's next week.

Wrinkly NAF suggests that the reason you find it so hard to fall asleep is because you're getting older and you'll never enjoy a good night's sleep the way you used to. It also reminds you that a sleepless night is bad for your complexion and that when you look in the mirror in the morning you'll see a few new wrinkles.

Kiddimus NAF fills your head with worries because your son still hasn't come home from his night out, and it reminds you that he's driving the family car, is probably tired, and could fall asleep at the wheel.

And, last but not least, your **"Look At Who You Married!"** NAF is on the warpath, suggesting that it's your husband's fault that you can't fall asleep because he's snoring so loudly. Your **"And, what on earth are you doing with him anyway?"** NAF reminds you what a hunk he used to be, and *"look how he ended up."* My advice for all these recurring situations is: prevention is better than cure!

Prepare a list of topics to think about if you wake up in the middle of the night and feel the frenzy of your NAFs coming on, you can decide that if you wake up you'll think about the sea, the waves, the soft sand, and the warm sun caressing you. Imagine the fish in the sea, and yourself sitting on the shore with a refreshing drink in your hand, examining seashells. You could think about a wonderful experience from the past and recall it in minute detail. It might seem a little bit artificial at first, but if you keep it up you'll be pleasantly surprised to discover yourself flowing with pleasurable thoughts, and it will become part of your routine. Choose whichever interesting/calming/happy subject comes into your head and you will discover that sleepless nights don't have to tortuous, and you might eventually fall asleep.

7. Knock on Wood – Ward off the Evil Eye

Getting rid of a familiar fear: the last technique to practice thinking enabling thoughts that attract a positive reality.

Okay, let's be honest. How many of us are simply afraid to think positively?

How many of us are afraid to admit to ourselves that our lives are basically quite good?

How many of us shy away from being happy in our heart of hearts? And why? Because we are afraid of the Evil Eye.

We're afraid to allow ourselves happiness, peace, and calm – afraid to attract a positive reality into our lives – because of one very stubborn NAF known as the **Evil Eye NAF**. **Evil Eye NAF** makes us say things like, "At least we're healthy, touch wood," and reminds us that everything is temporary, that today's situation could change tomorrow. **Evil Eye NAF** makes us secretive about how much we paid for our new home, so our friends won't know how much money we have and "put the Evil Eye" on us.

Evil Eye NAF makes us squirm when people compliment our children. Who knows what they'll be like as teenagers?

And it is the self-same NAF who makes us afraid to be happy, for fear that something bad might happen later.

Well ladies, I have news for you! The **Evil Eye NAF** is just another NAF. It lives in our heads and is a figment of our imagination. Therefore, you can use all the codes you've learned to deal with this NAF as well.

First of all, to weaken your **Evil Eye NAF**, I recommend that you start to practice being happy and enjoying the little things that bring you joy. This means being content in your heart and soul. Just like Pollyanna, try being grateful for all the good things in your life, and you will be surprised to see just how many good things there are. Touch wood…

Action Steps- A Moment With NAF

When you read about the latent potential of your thoughts, your NAF will probably start jumping up and down, demanding to be heard. So go ahead, let it out of the bag, once and for all.

Write down what your NAF is saying to you

_____

_____

_____

_____

What are your other voices saying?

_____

_____

_____

_____

_____

What is a "Stifling Thought"?

Did you ever stop to think about how we know what we know? The answer is obvious: experience, self-learning, formal education, practice, thinking. We believe the things we read or hear.

All these things shape who and what we are, for better or for worse. But sometimes, hidden in the piles of knowledge we've accumulated, we've got what are called "stifling thoughts."

Stifling thoughts consist of knowledge we have gathered that is based on false assumptions. One good metaphor is a house built of sponges rather than bricks. Like the house, these thoughts are not very stable.

We sometimes have every good intention to do something, but we never follow through. Why does that happen? We all have stifling thoughts that collide with our intentions. When the stifling thoughts are stronger than the action we intended on performing, we end up not performing the action. We're stuck. The stifling thoughts generate negative energy that contradicts the positive energy created by our original thought. It stifles our intended action or causes us to act against our true will. In other words, our stifling thought causes us to attract the things we don't want into our lives rather than the things we want!

We must pinpoint our stifling thoughts and understand that they are based on false assumptions. It's crucial to know that this type of thinking feeds our NAF and provides fertile ground for its growth. Most important, we must understand that stifling thoughts destroy enabling thoughts – thoughts that enable us to create and attract a positive reality for ourselves.

But don't worry. There's light at the end of the tunnel. The Law of Attraction doesn't act according to the vibes we sent out five minutes, five months, or five years ago. It operates on the vibes we're sending out right now. By identifying our stifling thoughts, and choosing thoughts that create a positive reality, we change the vibes we send from negative to positive and change our thoughts from stifling to enabling.

The following are examples of stifling thoughts that are based on false assumptions:

A stifling thought that ignores the present:

A thought that prevents us from living in the present, based on the false assumption that in the past everything was rosy and wonderful. A fantasy, a midsummer night's dream, forever young. This thought keeps us from experiencing what is happening at the moment. We never take the time to smell those flowers. We are afraid of what the present has to offer.

A stifling thought that prevents change:

A thought that causes us to resist change or makes it difficult for us to adapt to change. It's based on the false assumption that stability can be achieved in this world. No way! Our fear of change sometimes prevents us from entering certain situations or taking advantage of certain opportunities.

A stifling thought that compels results:

We can't always force the outcome exactly the way we wish. This is a thought that blinds us by making us certain that our efforts will lead to the desired results. When was the last time you tried to do something, over and over, so many times that you felt you were banging your head against the wall? Still, success escaped you. The thought is based on the false assumption that if you behave in a particular fashion you are bound to achieve the desired result. How could it be otherwise if you're the one in control? In reality however, things just happen, and we don't always have full control over them. If we take a deep breath and can pause for a while, the result or solution will come to us one way or another. Or, perhaps, we'll need to alter or replace the goal we were aiming for.

A stifling thought that restricts beliefs:

This type of thought leads us to believe that taking a particular course of action will produce only one possible result. It is based on the false assumption that only one outcome is possible if we act in a particular way. For example: "If I work outside the home, I'll become a terrible mother." "If I enroll in that course I'm interested in, I won't have time for my housework." "If I want to work from home, I'll have to give up my profession."

A stifling thought that exaggerates what others tell us:

This is a thought that makes us blow the things other people tell us way out of proportion, and even makes us believe that what happened to them will happen to us. It's based on the false assumption that we are directly affected by everything we hear. For example, a friend tells us she's sick and we immediately start feeling the same symptoms.

A stifling thought that represses feelings:

A thought that keeps us from fully feeling and experiencing things.

A stifling thought that leads us to be judgmental:

A thought that stifles our acceptance of others and leads us to judge and criticize them.

A stifling thought that limits development:

This thought makes us unable to express ourselves, grow, and progress.

A stifling thought that disregards other perspectives:

This thought keeps us from viewing events and people from different perspectives.

And that's only a partial list. We are plagued with many, many stifling thoughts. The accompanying workbook contains special exercises designed to confront our stifling thoughts. It offers techniques for identifying these thoughts in ourselves and the false assumptions on which they're based.

And now, as promised, my tips for Code No. 3 – "The Power of Thought"

Tip 1 – Look at the wrapper, not what's inside (really)

Quite often we obsess over things. An overweight woman might look critically at every other woman she sees on the street, checking out every part of her body from her backside to her thighs and breasts, and ask herself "Am I fatter than she is?" Naturally, **Fatso NAF** will be ready and waiting: *"Of course you're fatter than her, by far!"* This nasty but addictive little habit nearly ruins our self-esteem and our mood.

Try the following exercise:

Every time **Fatso NAF** (or any other NAF for that matter) makes you compare yourself to someone else, try and divert that thought in another direction. Check out the other woman's clothes to see if they match your taste. Look at her shoes and try to guess what she paid for them. In other words, if you have a tendency to compare yourself to other women, don't waste your time fighting it. But check out only things you're not sensitive about. You'll be surprised how effective and calming it can be (to look at the wrapper and not what's inside).

Tip 2 – Look in the Mirror and Smile

None of us is perfect, and at one time or another we are all dissatisfied with our appearance. But if this dissatisfaction becomes an obsession and the **Ugly Bug NAF** takes control, our good points will be totally camouflaged.

I suggest that you try the following exercise as a deterrent:

Every morning, after you've washed your face, look in the mirror, smile, and focus only on your favorite part of your face – the part you take pride in and have no complaints about. Don't look too closely, and don't start checking to see the state of your wrinkles. If you find yourself doing that, divert your eyes from the mirror immediately.

Find that satisfying feature, and a smile will brighten your eyes and give your cheeks a rosy glow, and your mood will improve – instantly.

Tip 3 – Prepare a list of goals and objectives for every mundane task

We all have routine chores that we're saddled with each and every day, things we do automatically and barely think about. Washing dishes, folding laundry, walking the dog... (even if your husband shares responsibility for them – and if he doesn't, it's high time he started!).

These tasks are a fertile breeding ground for our NAFs.

If you prepare yourself a list of goals to accomplish while you do each chore (goals that are totally unrelated to the task at hand), you'll soon see that you not only enjoyed the chore, and completed it quickly, but that it also served a useful purpose.

A woman who attended one of my workshops told me she'd decided to write a book. Though the desire to write had long burned inside her, she had no free time to come up with creative ideas. To her chagrin, her housekeeper quit and she became stuck with all the household chores. But every time she started a new task, she made herself a list of goals and objectives: "For the next half hour, while I wash these dishes, I'm going to come up with one great idea for my book. And by the end of the week, I'm going to outline the whole chapter…"

You can guess what happened – this woman's book is now nearly finished!

P.S. Now that you've cracked Code No. 3 – The Power of Thought, don't forget to open the accompanying workbook to the third chapter and pamper yourself with some more "attractive" exercises!

CHAPTER 4

CRACKING CODE NO. 4 – "LISTEN TO YOUR BODY"

"The body never lies."

—MARTHA GRAHAM

So, what can we expect by cracking the fourth Code of the Law of Attraction – "Listen to Your Body"?

We will learn that our body is our best friend. We will learn how to focus on what our body is feeling and trust our intuition, both of which will make us better able to attract. We will learn how to listen to our sensations and allow them to guide us, how to diminish that uneasy feeling, and how to loosen our NAFs' hold over us. We will get tips and action steps on how to make difficult decisions by relying on our body and our intuition.

Before we start cracking Code No. 4, "Listen to your Body," I'd like you to answer the following questions as honestly as you can:

Action Steps- Start Understanding your Connection with your Body

1. Does your body support you all the time, in everything you do? Or does it sometimes work against you?

2. To what extent do you feel that you live mainly according to your "head" and have distanced yourself from your body and what it feels?

3. Does your body "talk" to you? If so, how much do you listen to it?

With Whom Should you Have a Passionate Romance?

Have you ever thought about what it would be like to have a passionate romance with... your own body?

What would it be like to love your body totally and uncritically, respecting and appreciating it, understanding it, and devoting yourself to it?

Did you ever think about going out to have fun, just you and your body, without worrying about what you look like?

How would it be to listen to your body, be considerate of it, touch it, share your feelings with it, and listen to its advice?

Our body - that thin/fat/round/bony/tall/short/young/old body - is our active and dynamic partner throughout our lives, and it cooperates with us (or at least tries to) through thick and thin, even if we are not always aware of it.

Even our manner of speaking reflects our body's effect on our lives. We use expressions like "butterflies in my stomach," "a tightness in my throat," "a weight on my chest," "a heavy hand," and "body heat." These sensations are our body's attempts to talk to us, and listening to what it says can work wonders.

But, sadly, things are easier in theory than in practice. Most of us tend to ignore the messages our bodies send us, which represses our vitality and prevents us from enjoying life to the fullest. We, like so many others, have been influenced by Western culture, which has lost the connection between body and soul. The message we get from society is that our minds are supreme and our bodies are simply machines, like all the other mechanical devices in our lives.

Have you ever thought about the times you feel exhausted and withered, as if you're operating on an empty tank?

We most often feel this way when we do something we think we should be doing, or are obliged to do, whether we want to or not. We feel this way when, without being in touch with our body, our feelings, and our emotions, we are prisoners to what others say or how they perceive us.

On the other hand, when do we feel vital and full of energy?

When we are aware of our emotions and in touch with our true feelings. When we do what we actually enjoy doing and really want to do.

What's the Connection between your NAF, your Body and your Ability to Attract?

The more deeply we are sucked into the spiral of negative thoughts, the more detached we become from our bodies and from our body's internal balance. If we can ignore our NAF's manipulations, listening to our bodies will connect us to the present and to our inner feelings. Our bodies, as they say, never lie.

We all have negative thoughts passing through our minds, but not every negative thought is a NAF. Our NAFs become NAFs only when our bodies cooperate with them. Our NAF's energy is overwhelming. It takes control of us and our sensations for evil purposes. **"What Will They Say?" NAF,** for example, causes anyone with test anxiety to black out, start sweating and feeling a rapidly rising heart rate. **Hypochondriac NAF** gives headaches to anyone waiting for the results of a regular medical checkup. **Failure NAF** brings stomach aches, and sometimes runny bowels, to those who have an important task the following day. In other words, the body is a seismograph sensitive to all the struggles within it. The signals it sends can be extremely valuable. They can help us understand what is happening to us and direct our actions. And, of course, they can help us attract the things we truly want to bring into our lives. At any given moment, by identifying the sensations we are experiencing we can know if the vibes we are sending out are negative or positive. These sensations determine the type of vibes we project, as the following quote suggests:

"Good feels good. Bad feels bad." (Abraham-Hicks)

We sometimes have unpleasant thoughts for no particular reason – at least none we are aware of. For example, we may suffer from stomach discomfort, nervousness, or insomnia. Most times we ignore these sensations and continue functioning as usual. Our energy slowly but surely starts draining away, bit by bit, until it's totally depleted. No wonder we stop attracting the things we want and draw only undesirable elements into our lives.

Let's learn how to focus on the sensations in our body, how to listen to them, and how they can guide us into attracting into our lives what we truly desire. Let's learn how to take huge bites out of life and enjoy every mouthful!

How to live your life to the fullest (rather than watching from the sidelines) by strengthening your link to your body's sensations

Imagine the following situation:

You are engrossed in something very important that demands total concentration, and your young daughter wants your attention. You ignore her and try to concentrate on what you are doing. Your daughter becomes annoyed and starts to nag. You can no longer concentrate on the task at hand but are determined to carry on and not give in to her. As you feel your energy sapping away, you become angrier with your daughter, whose whining has now turned into an ear-splitting scream. You eventually realize that she will calm down only if you give her some attention, listen to her and try to understand what's bothering her, or find her something to occupy herself with. Only then will you be able to return to your task in peace and make some progress.

Does that sound familiar? And what if I tell you that the same thing is happening with your body?

The little girl in the story is our body, which tries in every possible way to make us aware that "all is not well." It wants our attention. Something is not quite right, but we just ignore it and carry on being busy. Our body continues to send its signals, which begin as little twinges and end up as serious pain. By that time we have no choice but to pay it some attention.. By then, however, it may be too late.

Many times we become hysterical over an unusual or unpleasant sensation and we invest all our energy in trying to avoid feeling it. We ignore that our heart is beating a little too fast, or that our stomach aches, or that our chest feels tight. We naively believe we can erase these unpleasant feelings by putting them out of our minds. We carry on putting our body through its paces as though it were a machine. We think that if we carry on as usual and ignore that tightness in our chest, it will go away.

But what actually happens?

When we ignore those unpleasant sensations, they don't go away.

They just grow stronger until eventually our body collapses.

Our repression of these sensations merely roots them even deeper, and they become even more troublesome. They want our attention. They want us to acknowledge their existence. They want us to listen to them, which is why they keep signaling to us that something is not quite right. If we repress these sensations, we lose contact with our bodies.

Strengthening our connection with our body and its sensations requires awareness, understanding, and practice. Here are five ways that significantly help the women I work with to strengthen each one's connection to her body and attract the things she really wants:

- Listen to your body.
- Involve your body in your decision-making process.
- Trust your intuition.
- Be aware of all information you receive, and examine your sensations.
- Duplicate the good sensations.

1. Listen to your body

The objective here is to help us practice paying attention to our bodies, to allow us - especially those of us who are ruled by our heads - to discover the world of our body.

So, how do we listen to our bodies?

The process is so simple. To be honest, you'll be surprised to learn just how simple it is, and you'll wonder why you never tried it before. All you need to do is be aware. As soon as we feel the beginning of an unpleasant sensation of tension or stress, we must act according to the Identification Code and distinguish between the sensation and the body itself.

Operating according to the Detachment Code, we separated our identity with our negative voice; we understood that it was just one of our many voices. In this case, we have to understand that the sensation is a warning about something happening inside us; it isn't us. We have to understand that the sensation exists because our bodies want to tell us something. Rather than letting the sensation take hold, we can simply pay attention to it.

We must try to focus on the sensation and understand what it wants to tell us - what led to its very existence. Just focusing on the sensation calms it down, and its hold over us begins to diminish. Sometimes this is just temporary relief and the sensation will return later, in force. Take this as a sign that something still requires our full and total attention.

Action Steps- Start Breathing

One way to practice concentrating on and listening to our body's sensations is to pay attention to our breathing. Breathing is a means of communicating with our bodies. It's a simple action that we perform nonstop, and it's our most important resource.

If you sense pressure in your stomach, try the following exercise:

Sit or lie down comfortably and concentrate solely on your breathing. Think only about breathing in and breathing out. Feel the temperature of the air entering your body and the temperature of the air you breathe out. The air is slightly colder as you breathe in, and slightly warmer as you breathe out. Take deep breaths. Breathe in through your nose, and exhale through your mouth.

After concentrating on your breathing for a few minutes, pay attention to your heart rate. Do you feel any kind of tension in your body - in your stomach, neck, shoulders?

Concentrate on the physical sensations in each part of your body. Focus on them for a while to see what happens. Think about these sensations as a secret letter addressed to you. If you are open-minded and curious enough the letter will open and you can read its message, intended solely for you.

Slowly and gently relax your arms at the sides of your body, rotate your shoulders, open your eyes, and continue breathing deeply.

Now, how does that feel?

Here is a fascinating story about listening to our body. Marion, one of my coachees, used to work for a very large international company. She was an executive with a great deal of responsibility on her shoulders. Gradually, she began to collapse under the stress of the job. She totally ignored all of her body's warning signals, which included many sleepless nights. After a while she started showing a very strange symptom. The skin on her hands began to peel, so much so that her raw flesh was exposed. Her hands looked like raw meat, and she couldn't even bear to touch a piece of paper or leaf through a book. She consulted the best dermatologists to try and find out what was causing the problem and how to solve it. But not one of them could discover the root of the problem. One evening, as she was sitting alone at home, she began to focus on her body's sensations, and suddenly she understood the reason. As if struck by a flash of lightning, she saw it all clearly. She knew that she could no longer carry on as she had been and that she had to take immediate action, even extreme action, to reduce her stress level and stop attracting only harmful things into her life.

Marion decided to give up her job to reduce the level of stress in her life. Guess what happened? Two days after she handed in her resignation the dryness on her hands cleared up and they returned to normal, with no need for doctors or medication.

This story is the best possible illustration of the concept that our body is our best friend. Our body knows what is best for us and tries to warn us when something goes wrong. Only by learning to listen to our body can we exploit this amazing tool and understand why it reacts the way it does. We can then not only calm our sensations but do something about what produces them.

Marion's body was signaling that she couldn't stand the stress she was being subjected to.

Its first signal was a general feeling of malaise, which Marion ignored.

Then it tried sleepless nights, which Marion ignored. Then it tried palpitations, which Marion also ignored.

Finally, when none of its tactics attracted any attention from Marion, it decided to issue its strongest warning yet. It deprived her of the use of her hands. She was unable to work, unable even to touch simple objects. Only then did Marion finally started listening to her body and understand that the solution was in her hands – literally!

2. Involve your body in the decision making process

Now that we understand how to pay attention to our body, we can go one step further and use our body to make important decisions. These are the decisions that help us attract what we truly desire, not the things our NAF tells us we need.

What does that mean in practical terms?

We have all, at one time or other, reached a crossroad in our lives when we have had to make a fateful decision. No matter how hard the decision, we know that once we've made it and are confident we were right, we will relax and be filled with the peaceful sensation that we made the right choice. Until we make that choice however, we go through purgatory.

Our NAFs overtake our minds and our bodies, bringing trouble no matter which path we choose. We go backwards and forwards, changing our minds all the time, unable to make a conclusive decision. We become obsessed with the problem morning, noon and night. We are unable to concentrate on other things and have no idea what to do.

This is where our faithful old friend, our body, comes into the picture. Our body is our best source of information. Our body knows better than anyone what is best for us (and not what is best for those around us). Our body knows our Inner Core, what our heart desires – even if we have worked hard to repress and hide this information over the years. Our body never lies to us, and we can use our body's vast knowledge to make difficult decisions.

Sarah's Story

Sarah and her family relocated from France to the U.S. because of her husband's job. He was offered an opportunity to manage a large branch of an international retail chain, and, like many other couples, Sarah and her husband decided that the offer was too good to pass up and that they would try their luck in America. Sarah was faced with an enormous change in her life, having built her home and raised her family in Paris. She was about to leave her relatives, her good friends, and her familiar routine and culture. She had no idea how much she would come to miss all those things.

Before they left for the U.S., Sarah held an enormous yard sale, and in one fell swoop she sold the entire contents of her home, essentially wiping out her past. She sold furniture, ornaments, items of sentimental value to her and her family. Busy as she was with the sale and the move, Sarah didn't really think about the next stage, or even about how she and the family would react to the sale of all their property and the obliteration of their past. She was engrossed in convincing potential purchasers why they should buy a particular plant or carpet.

By the end of the sale, the only things remaining in their home were their books and their professional equipment. And so, Sarah and her family moved to the U.S. and began a new chapter in their lives – in a foreign country, with a new language and unfamiliar culture, in an empty new house.

For the first few weeks after her arrival Sarah felt as though she lived in a bubble, as if she were watching her life from outside. Nothing was real to her. But after a month, suddenly everything changed. Her husband started his new job, her children went to school and to preschool, and Sarah, who had managed a busy department of a hi-tech company and had always had a full schedule and a busy life, suddenly found herself sitting alone in a strange house with nothing to do, with no friends, no close family, and no familiar routine. Though she had always loved to dress well and go out to socialize, she now sat at home wearing a tracksuit and slippers. The woman who was used to knowing where she was going and what her next assignment would be began to sink in a whirlpool of uncertainty and negative thoughts. A chorus of NAFs began singing loudly in her head.

You'll Never Go Back NAF reminded her – morning, noon, and night – what a huge mistake she'd made by moving to the States and how she would never return home to France. They had no return date in mind, and as time passed they sensed they might reach the point of no return.

"You left the country. You left and you deserted all your friends and relatives!" Her NAF's words echoed in her ears, giving Sarah no peace. *"What about your children? They will grow up as Americans. Your children, the fruit of your womb, will become foreigners to you. And how will they learn and remember their mother tongue? They won't know how to read and write in French. And what about your extended family? When will you see them again? From now on, you'll see your relatives twice a year, at most. Your children won't know their grandparents. You won't be there to celebrate birthdays and other landmark occasions. You won't be around to share the good times or the bad."*

Careeristus NAF claimed she was wasting her potential: *"Look at who you were in France, and look at yourself now. Your entire career is going down the drain. Why did you bother studying for so* *many years? What is the point of all your professional experience if all you do is sit at home, doing 'nothing'."*

Nostalgia NAF reminded her how wonderful things were "back home" compared with their current life in the U.S. It painted their former life in pastel colors and reminded her relentlessly of the friends they had left behind, of the family trips and outings. Everything was so inviting and familiar back home, and now she was in a foreign country that felt strange and cold.

Sarah decided it was time for action – she had to find a job. She began to look for a suitable position in her field but found nothing. And so several years went by. Sarah gave birth to another child, which further decreased her chances of finding a job. After five years in the U.S., Sarah and her family decided they would return to France the following summer. Their time in the States had served its purpose, and they missed their home and their relatives too much to stay away any longer. They notified everyone that they'd be home within a few months.

But then, suddenly, after she'd given up finding a suitable job, Sarah received a very tempting offer to manage the local branch of a hi-tech company.

The offer took her completely by surprise. Sarah was engrossed in preparations for the move back home that she'd been dreaming about for so long. And now, suddenly, she received this offer, which, if it had come a year earlier, she would have accepted with open arms. The timing changed the whole picture and left Sarah feeling confused and dejected. She faced the hardest decision of her life. Should she accept this exciting offer and advance her career, gain experience, earn a good salary, and generally feel she had "made it" in America? Or should she do what she had wanted to do for so long – return home where she belonged, to those she loved and missed so much, but without a job, and with the feeling that she had failed?

Sarah didn't know what to do. Unsettled and unable to concentrate, she was beset by sleepless nights. She had no patience for her husband or her children, even though they were willing to support whatever decision she made. Sarah made a list of the pros and cons of each option but was still unable to decide. At a point when her anxiety had grown almost too great to bear, she showed up at my workshop.

In the course of the workshop I suggested to Sarah that she concentrate on the sensations in her body. I explained the concept of our bodies being our best friends that know what is right for us – the reality that we want to attract into our lives. Her body would light the way and show her which option to choose. After I explained to her, step by step, what she had to do, Sarah went home to do her homework.

The next day, she came back with tears in her eyes and told me how she had applied the Listen to your Body Code and made a crucial decision:

Sarah explained that she'd gone home and made sure that the house was quiet, with no children around and no noise to distract her. She turned out the lights in her bedroom and lay on her bed. She began to breathe deeply to relax her body, and she drifted into thought…

She began by imagining that she had decided to accept the tempting offer to stay in the U.S. She imagined herself sitting in her fantastic office in Manhattan, conducting a business meeting, while a babysitter was taking care of her new baby. She saw herself in her successful career, wearing fancy business suits, lap-top in hand, and meeting people all the time. As she visualized all of this, Sarah concentrated on the sensations in her body. To her amazement, Sarah experienced feelings she had never imagined. She felt as though her entire body was shrinking, becoming wrinkled and shriveled, until she sensed she was as small as a raisin. At the same time, every part of her body seemed to weigh a ton. Her arms and her legs felt too heavy to move. It was such an unpleasant feeling that Sarah forcefully shook herself to return back to reality.

Next, she imagined deciding to turn down the offer and follow through on her plans to return to France. She imagined exactly how it would feel to go back home, to land at the airport, to see all her friends and relatives waiting for her. She imagined inviting them to dinner, spending time with her friends, taking the children to the beach, speaking her native tongue with ease and with everyone, and living the life she loved and missed. Again, Sarah concentrated on the sensations in her body, and, again, was amazed at her reaction. She felt as though her entire body was streaming with energy. She felt her muscles get stronger and her heart beat faster due to all the excitement, and that's when the answer became clear. She knew what would make her feel happy and fulfilled. She decided to return back home - to France!

Action Steps – How to Use your Body in the Decision-Making Process

1. Clearly define the factors that are hindering your decision-making process.

2. Arrange for a relaxing atmosphere: make sure the house is quiet, lie down in a darkened room with nothing to disturb you.

3. Breathe in deeply several times to relax yourself, and commence the process.

4. Imagine yourself having chosen the first option. What are you doing? What are you wearing? How do you act? Think about all the good things that will result from this option, ignore the negative aspects, and don't think about the second option.

5. Concentrate on the physical sensations and pay attention to how you feel. You can use images, feelings, emotions – anything that works. You can describe your sensations as if you were an object or a child, for instance.

6. Now imagine yourself in the second situation, having chosen the second option. What are you doing? What are you wearing? How do you act? Again, you must only think about the good things that will result from this option, ignore the negative aspects, and not think about the first option.

7. Concentrate on your physical sensations and how you feel this time. Again, image, feelings, and emotions are all acceptable tools.

8. Make your decision, smile, and pamper yourself with a massage – you deserve it!

3. Trust your Intuition

Sometimes our bodies communicate with us through a fleeting spark of brilliance, a "click" of total understanding. This momentary flicker of light is called intuition.

Some people regard intuition as an unripe, undeveloped thought. It's that "Eureka!" moment when we suddenly realize that "That's it!" We understand what we have to do. We can't explain how and why; we just know.

Our intuition can guide us as we take the next step, warn us about what's ahead, lead us along the path. It can direct us to specific destinations and show us where our best chances of success lie. Even if we can't fully explain it, intuition sometimes acts as an alarm bell. I am prepared to wager with you that your intuition has never let you down.

But, do we trust our intuition and allow it to guide us? The answer is, NO!

Why do we prefer to heed our logical voice rather than rely on our intuition?

Because we know that if we act according to our intuition, we will be "punished."

Because we were brought up to do "the right thing," rather than what our intuition tells us.

If we are sometimes tempted to rely on our intuition, we find the prospect frightening. The frenzy of our NAFs begins: "It's not worth trying. You'll never succeed. And just think what people will say."

We may suddenly remember situations when we acted according to our intuition and failed. Or we may find it's been so long since we followed our intuition that we've forgotten how to use it, and that when we do have a flash of intuition we might not even recognize it.

Women's intuitions are better than men's for the things most women value: home, family and children, couplehood. Most men have better intuitions for work and career-related matters. It's a shame that we women don't use our intuition more in the business world. We don't dare use it in "men's" areas for fear that people will say we're being guided by emotion rather than logic.

My advice to you is: Start acting on your intuition! Your intuition doesn't make mistakes. It knows what you want and what is best for you.

When we ignore our intuition, we end up settling for less. We have doubts. We feel we can't trust ourselves. And we end up making wrong decisions.

No one else has access to your intuition, only you. Therefore, no one else can advise you not to act on your intuition.

Action Steps – A Moment With Your NAF

When you read about the power of intuition, your NAF is probably jumping up and down, shouting: "Ha!!! Do you remember what happened last time you acted on your intuition? What a slap in the face that was!"

Take a few minutes to try and remember, and write down exactly why you felt so disappointed after following your intuition:

_____

_____

_____

_____

_____

_____

I suggest that you start following your intuition. Learn to listen to it, and make it work for you! But remember that you must do this responsibly, with a minimum of risk. I don't mean that you should drop everything now and start acting. But simply being aware of your intuition and understanding why it is important to you is a crucial stage in finding a solution and arriving at a decision. With correct planning, you can accomplish this with minimal risk.

Action Steps – Project the Mental Scenario You Want

It may be so long since we relied on our intuition that we can't even recognize it. All we need to do is be aware.

When you have to do something, or make any sort of decision, try to act on your intuition. Go with your gut feeling.

If you see, in retrospect, that your intuition was correct, try to remember how you discovered it and how you felt relying on it. In other words, try to notice when and how your intuition appeared. Did you feel palpitations, a rush of energy, a tingling feeling in your stomach?

Your intuition can make itself known in different ways. It's worth learning to recognize when and how it appears.

4. Be Aware of All Information, and Check out Your Feelings

No matter what your daily agenda is like - busy, calm, interesting, boring - be aware of all information coming your way via e-mail, telephone, or any other source that makes you feel excited or happy, even if the feeling lasts only a moment. That sensation is actually your intuition, signaling that something good is happening to you here.

Your intuition is the keyhole to the door that will open before you, revealing positive opportunities. It shows us we're capable of attracting positive things into our lives. Pay attention to the vibes that are awakening you to life. It is these vibes that make you attractive - they allow you to attract the things you desire!

5. Duplicate That Positive Sensation

Did you ever think about the true meaning of the word "plenty?" Is "plenty" an objective concept meaning that nothing is lacking? Or, does it indicate a sensation? Well, I've got news for you. "Plenty" is something we sense!

When we feel we've got plenty, we feel great. As a consequence, we send out positive vibes and, of course, become more attractive – attracting into our lives the reality we long for. When we set out for an exciting trip, are about to enter an interesting meeting, or are due for a raise in salary, we feel the satisfaction of having plenty; even though we haven't yet left for the trip, gone to the meeting, or received the pay raise. Just knowing these events will take place very shortly does wonders for us – even before we see the actual results.

Plenty, then, is a feeling. And my claim is that we can deliberately duplicate that feeling – double it for extra effect. When we become excited over the anticipation of something positive, we project positive vibes outward and attract more "plenty" into our lives. The greater our ability to attract, the more "plentiful" the results.

Therefore, to fortify your connection with your body, and at the same time strengthen your ability to attract the positive, think about what gives you a good sensation, a feeling of plenty. Try to reproduce that sensation so that it occurs more and more frequently in your daily life. This is the key to projecting more positive vibes and attracting even stronger sensations of plenty. Simply put, you'll just feel better.

And now, as promised, my tips for Code No. 4 – "Listen to Your Body"

Tip 1 – Hug Yourself

Knowing that our body is our very best friend, and understanding that our body is constantly performing thousands of essential functions simultaneously, we have good reason to be pleased with our body and to be grateful for it.

Stand at ease, with your legs together and your arms hanging freely at your sides. Breathe deeply, moving your head, shoulders, and arms in a circular pattern.

Now, stroke your face, your forehead, and your scalp. Massage your scalp, and then move on to massage your legs. Give yourself an enormous hug. When was the last time you hugged yourself and gave your body this much attention? You deserve it, and so does your body!

Tip 2 – Loosen Up

I recommend that you try this exercise when you are home alone.

Stand at ease, with your legs together and your arms hanging freely at your sides. Breathe deeply, moving your head, shoulders, and arms in a circular pattern.

Pound your chest with your fists, and make noises like a monkey in the jungle. It might feel a bit embarrassing at first, but the reason will soon become clear.

Increase the volume of your monkey noises, louder and louder until you are shouting. Don't worry: the walls absorb all the noise, and your body is being cleansed.

After pounding for a few moments and making all the noise you possibly can, relax your arms, relax your shoulders, move your head in a circular pattern, breathe deeply, and go on with your day.

Tip 3 – Start a New Habit...

Take a minute out of your regular routine, in-between all the running around, chores, meetings, etc. Train yourself to stop and start a new habit – breathe deeply. Two minutes, no more than that, is all you need to become aware of your feelings and to reconnect with your body. Now you can carry on with whatever it is you were doing!

P.S. Now that you've cracked Code No. 4 – Listen To Your Body, don't forget to open the accompanying workbook to the fourth chapter and pamper yourself with some more "attractive" exercises!

CHAPTER 5

CRACKING CODE NO. 5 – YOUR ENVIRONMENT

"Keep away from people who try to belittle your ambitions. Small people always do that, but the really great make you feel that you, too, can become great."

—MARK TWAIN

> **So, what can we expect by cracking the fifth Code of the Law of Attraction – "Your Environment"?**
>
> You will be surprised to learn the extent to which we are shaped by our environment. We will learn to recognize and analyze the elements of our environment. We will learn how we can change our environment so that it stops bringing us down and begins pulling us upward. We will get tips and action steps on how to set boundaries, how to rid ourselves of our "energy drainers," and how to increase our intake of "energy snacks."

What is Our Environment?

Have you ever thought why we sometimes arrive at places energized and full of vigor, but within minutes we want to turn round, go home and crawl back into bed? Have you ever found yourselves abandoning a new and exciting idea, just because a "good friend" trashed it? Did you ever read an article in the newspaper that excited you so much that you wanted to learn more about the topic?

These are just some indications of the immense influence our environment has on us – on our mood, our energy, and our motivation – and on our ability to attract what we truly desire.

The environment in which we live shapes our behavior patterns and dictates what is expected of us: how we should look, what is acceptable and what is not, what is fashionable, what is polite. It teaches us how to distinguish right from wrong, when to act, when to refrain from acting, when to compromise...

Most of us consider our environment a "given" that we must accept for what it is. We've got to live with it and make the best of it. We are not at all aware of its great influence, particularly on how we react to other people and, most importantly, on ourselves. We are unaware that our environment has the capacity to bring us down or pull us up and support us along the way. Or that it can put negative thoughts in our heads and compound the influence of our NAFs, at the same time filling us with a sense of security, love, stability, and appreciation.

So what is this environment that has such a significant influence on our lives, and primarily on our thoughts?

We can categorize it along the following three planes:

- Human environment
- Physical environment
- Conceptual environment

1. Human Environment

This is the environment of family, friends, colleagues, and neighbors – basically all the people around us with whom we have contact. Sometimes, though neither they nor we are aware of it, these people exert social pressure and have a negative influence on us. They continually convey their personal expectations and let us know what they believe to be the "right thing." We react and try to adapt ourselves to their views. Too often every single thing we do is in some way connected to our preoccupation with *"What will 'they' think of us?" "What will 'they' say?"* How will what we do be accepted by society?

We often find ourselves surrounded by people who do not appreciate what we do or respect what is important to us. They don't allow us to grow, develop, and fulfill our desires and loves – the elements of our Inner Core. Sometimes just being in the company of these people drains us of so much energy. It weakens and agonizes us, but, most significantly, it feeds our NAFs.

In the work environment, most female managers of large organizations and companies are aware that the prevailing organizational culture is male-oriented. Some women in key management positions have a sense of solitude and dissatisfaction in the upper echelons.

Men and women relate in completely different ways to situations in their places of work and in their careers, with regard to office politics, the threat of competition, delegation of responsibility, supervision of subordinates, teamwork etc. Our work environment can greatly affect how we feel about our jobs, how we see ourselves, advance our careers, and attract what we want (or, sometimes what we don't want).

The following fable illustrates the point nicely:

Once upon a time there was a frog race. The first frog to reach the top of a tall tower would be the winner. Many people gathered to watch the race, even though they didn't really believe the frogs had any chance at all of reaching the top. The spectators could even be heard murmuring: *"It's pointless. They'll never succeed!"*

Slowly but surely, frog after frog gave up. The spectators kept saying, *"You see, it's really a waste of time. They'll never make it!"* In the end, all the frogs dropped out of the race, except for one lone female frog, who finally, with great effort, reached the top of the tower. The other frogs were amazed and dying to know how she did it. One of them approached her to ask for her secret and found out that... she was deaf! The point of the fable is that you should always turn a deaf ear to people who tell you that you'll never be able to fulfill your dreams!

And, as long as we're talking about our ability to attract, everyone we attract into our lives and relationships is connected with something we project, either consciously or subconsciously. If we want to know what it is, exactly, that we're projecting, all we have to do it take a look at the people we've attracted. Usually, there's a connection; these people will be similar in nature to the vibes (either negative or positive) that we're sending out to our environment. Ideally, we aspire to be strong, optimistic, and happy people, and to attract others who have these same qualities. When this happens, we feel great – confident and content. On the other hand, when we feel depressed and let our NAFs rules our lives, we're sending out negative vibes and attracting people who are chronic complainers. The reason is simple. These types of people are transmitting the same vibes we are. They are the people who pull us down, often pulling themselves down in the process. Synergy then takes place, and the combined effect of the negative vibes pulls us even further down.

2. Physical Environment

Our physical environment is, in order of importance, our home (our "private temple"), our office or workplace, our town, and our state or country. Our home is our refuge, but is it always the metaphoric "fortress?" How do we feel about the place where we spend so much of our time? Are we comfortable there? Have we created a welcoming and warm atmosphere that reflects who we really are? It is very important that we answer these questions in the affirmative.

A participant in one of my workshops told me that she hated the apartment that she'd moved into six months earlier. When we asked her why, she replied that the apartment had no sense of order. She could never find anything, and instead of being able to control the mess, the mess controlled her. She was beset by pangs of conscience because every morning she decided that "today was the day" she was going to tidy up and organize everything, but by the end of the day she'd supplied endless excuses for not doing it. The result was that she was living in a place that made her feel bad. More importantly, however, the state of disorder in her apartment had an overall negative influence that contributed to her general feeling of unease. These are the vibes she projected outward, which impaired her ability to attract what she truly desired.

3. Conceptual Environment

Our conceptual environment includes television, newspapers, computers and Internet, ads and commercials, books, courses, games, toys – anything and everything that stimulates our thoughts and intellect. The media play a significant role in our environment.

We can see, for example, how our conceptual environment gives our **UglyBug NAF** fertile ground for planting its negative thoughts. A recent commercial for a certain brand of ice cream featured a beautiful, slender (of course) model wearing tight jeans and licking an enticing looking chocolate cone. The floor around her was littered with seven empty wrappers, while three unopened ice cream cones waited for her on the table. Does that situation sound realistic? Logical? Think about what that sort of commercial does to us average female viewers. What feelings does it stir up?

We will never, but never, attain the dimensions of that model, not even if we diet for months. How unfair can life be? How can she possibly gorge herself on ten ice cream cones and still look like a million dollars, while we can't even allow ourselves one measly cone. And if we do give in to temptation, we're overtaken by guilt feelings that drain all the enjoyment out of that one sweet moment!

How are we supposed to feel good about ourselves when we see a commercial like that, or when the only guests on talk shows are beautiful models, rich businesspeople, and accomplished politicians – people who've "made it?" Is this an ideal society that reinforces our self-confidence in our femininity? Or is it a perfect yet unobtainable reality that the media set out to portray?

Did you ever think about how early our brainwashing begins? Even little girls are being brainwashed as they play with their Barbie dolls – the original "supermodel." Have you ever stopped to think about what Barbie actually looks like? Well, I have news for you. Barbie has exactly the "right" proportions – a narrow waist, tight round buttocks, and, of course, a pair of perfect breasts that any plastic surgeon would be proud of. She has long, wavy blond hair, and beautiful blue eyes. That is the Barbie doll we played with, and we buy the same doll for our own daughters. Barbie never ages; she will always remain twenty years old.

Barbie has undergone a few changes over the years to adapt her to changing fashions. In the 1970s and '80s, when smaller breasts were fashionable, Barbie's breasts were small and pert, like a pair of perky plums. With the changing fashion for larger breasts beginning in the mid-'90s, Barbie suddenly sported fuller breasts the size of firm and plump grapefruits

And we remain silent. We buy push-up bras, try on clothes, make an effort to stay eternally young, slim, and beautiful. The cosmetic surgery industry goes wild and so does the frenzy of our NAFs.

So why do we put up with all this? Why do we accept our environment as a "given" that we cannot change? There is so much we can do to improve our environment, to change it and shape it to positive influence our lives. So why don't we just do it?

If we just understand the vast influence that our environment has on us, we can exclude the elements that hold us back; we can introduce elements that support our efforts to fulfill our Inner Core and attract its positive elements into our lives.

It's not complicated. We just need the will to understand what we need to do and how to go about doing it.

How can you change your environment so that rather than bringing you down, it pulls you up and supports you along the way?

I offer you three effective means to this end:

- Define boundaries
- Get rid of your "energy drainers"
- Add "energy snacks"

1. Learn to Set Boundaries

The first step toward designing our own environment is to learn to set boundaries. These are the invisible lines we draw around ourselves – a defense mechanism to ward off people who behave toward us in ways we consider inappropriate.

These boundaries help us define who we are, how far we are prepared to go, and how far we will allow other people into our physical and emotional territory. They determine what we can request or even demand of others without feeling guilty or uncomfortable.

Most importantly, defining boundaries enables us to feel good about ourselves, to protect us from insult and injury. We must set boundaries for concepts as well as for people, and forbid entry to anything we see as contradicting our values, draining our energy, and preventing us from accomplishing our goals.

So... what am I taking about?

Sophie's story is an excellent example. Sophie and Amanda are best friends, bosom buddies. Every time Sophie is aggravated, insulted, angry, or simply upset she shares her feelings with Amanda. Her friend then nods sympathetically, adds her comments, and fuels Sophie's fire.

When Sophie told Amanda that she'd been insulted by a mutual friend, Amanda said it was a terrible thing and that Sophie should never forgive her. She also reminded Sophie of an earlier incident when the mutual friend behaved shamefully toward her.

When Sophie told Amanda that she'd started ceramics classes and had made her first vase, Amanda responded by telling her friend that she had never had any artistic talent and would be better off finding "some other nonsense" to fill her time.

When Sophie came to Amanda to confide her marital problems, Amanda nodded and told her that the situation would never improve and that the best thing for Sophie would be to separate from her husband as soon as possible.

Whether Amanda was right or wrong, she had a devastating influence on Sophie. Instead of encouraging, supporting, and strengthening her good friend, Amanda was doing the opposite – feeding the NAFs in Sophie's heart. Sophie was stuck in a vicious cycle – perpetuating her dependence upon Amanda, continuing to let her enter her "borders," and, as a result, torturing her own battered ego. By the time Sophie told me about her long and enduring friendship with Amanda, she already knew what she needed to do. She understood that she had to be the one to define the boundaries, and not to allow Amanda to continue to be her confidant and her "closest friend." With a friend like Amanda, she certainly didn't need enemies!

Sophie knew that she had to define her boundaries, despite the unpleasantness it might involve.

We must also define boundaries in our human work environment.

In my coaching workshops for female executives in large organizations, I constantly stress that "You, as a female senior manager, can improve your achievements, increase the extent of your influence on the organization, and significantly improve your successful leadership qualities." All this can be achieved without having to "become a man" and without adopting management methods from a strictly male domain; you can succeed by defining your own boundaries and strengthening and deepening your feminine management techniques according to your Inner Core qualities.

We must remember that we are the ones who allow people to relate to us in the ways they do. We decide on the boundaries. The decision to latch onto someone else's negative vibes is entirely ours. Conversely, the decision to surround ourselves with people who do us good, and pull us upward, is also ours entirely. Don't forget: it's all a matter of choice!

It makes sense to define boundaries, not only for people but also for the conceptual and physical elements surrounding us. We must forbid entrance to anything that defeats us, disturbs our composure, and encourages our NAFs to go to work. On the other hand, we must open the gates to everything that encourages us, makes us feel good, and pulls us upward.

Judith's Story

Judith always dreamed that she would have a large family. She wanted four children – two boys and two girls.

When she was 27, Judith and her husband decided that it was time to have a baby. All Judith's friends were at the same stage in life: some were in the middle of their first pregnancy, others already had a newborn baby, and the rest were trying, like Judith, to conceive. Judith was surrounded by young mothers, rosy-cheeked babies, and a lot of noise and racket.

But Judith could not get pregnant. At first she thought it was just a matter of time, and that soon she would manage to conceive. But as the months passed, her heart filled with worry and her NAFs began their merry dance. **Kiddimus NAF** proclaimed that all her friends had babies and that she was the only one who didn't, which meant there was something wrong with her. It convinced her that she would never be a mother. **Kiddimus NAF** made Judith look longingly at every young mother she saw pushing a stroller down the street, and then to shed a secret tear.

Her **"What Will They Say?" NAF** warned her that she must keep her problems a secret from her family and friends because they would only feel sorry for her, and some of her friends might even stop seeing her or think she's strange. Family visits became a living nightmare for Judith. When her mother and her mother-in-law asked probing questions about when Judith and her husband planned to expand their family, Judith just forced a smile, and, guided by her **"What Will They Say?" NAF**, told them there was plenty of time and that it was more important to them to establish their careers first. Judith even had a hard time of it at work because she had to use office hours for appointments at the fertility clinic, and she needed to invent an elaborate excuse for her boss each time. **"What Will They Say?" NAF** told her that if her boss discovered the real reason, he would fire her. In the end, he did just that, on the grounds that she had no reasonable explanation for her many absences. Judith began to sit at home, day after day, coping alone with her fertility treatments, her fears, and her bleak thoughts. She pretended that everything was normal when she met her friends on social occasions, but she would cry herself to sleep at night. Her relationship with her husband also began to suffer. Her **"Look at who You Married" NAF** whispered to her that everything was his fault but reminded her that she was the one who had to suffer all the fertility treatments. To make matters worse, it told her that she was the only one who cared; her husband, it said, was not an active partner in the process, and he'd been spending much more time at work lately. Judith began to keep her distance from her family as well, and her face remained a closed book every time the subject was raised.

After five years of fertility treatments, Judith came to one of my workshops. I knew she would have to concentrate on changing her environment. Her first step was to change her physical environment. Judith found a part-time job, which enabled her to get out of the house and meet people, to be active, and most importantly to shoo her NAFs out of her head while she continued her fertility treatments.

Judith's second step was to change her human environment. She began to meet other women in her situation, and to discuss her feelings with them. Judith soon realized that she was not alone. There were many other women suffering from infertility, and there were different methods of coping. Hiding from others, she realized, was not the answer.

Judith's third step was to decide to ignore her **"What Will They**

Say?" **NAF** and to share her troubles with those around her. Instcad of hiding the true situation from her family and friends, Judith took action. She gathered her courage, stepped out of her comfort zone, and told them everything. As soon as the subject was no longer taboo, Judith felt an immense sense of relief and received much more warmth and support than she ever expected.

Judith's fourth and final step, which she took together with her husband, was to begin making enquiries at adoption agencies.

To her complete surprise, after taking all these positive steps, the stress and pressure Judith felt began to dissipate, and she saw a gleam of light at the end of the tunnel. Judith realized that, biologically or not, one day she would attract her greatest wish - a baby of her own.

Lyndsey's Story

Lyndsey grew up in a family that hid illness. They talked about it in hushed voices, behind closed doors - *"The neighbors must never know."* That is how Lyndsey came to grow up with an obsessive fear of cancer. Any pain, even the smallest twinge, became magnified in her imagination to the worst possible option. Her **Malignant NAF** worked around the clock and every night it would whisper new details and give her nightmares about illnesses.

In her mind's eye Lyndsey saw men, women, and children with shaven heads. Her NAF allowed her no rest and stressed her out before every medical examination. NAF even made Lyndsey wonder which of her parents' friends had fallen prey to cancer, how they discovered they were sick, what symptoms they felt, how they felt after the treatment, and what it did to their appearance.

Lyndsey knew that her time was limited. The sword of Damocles would land on her one day. It was only a matter of time …

Lyndsey began to work as a medical rep at a large pharmaceutical company. Since she was so interested in and knowledgeable about cancer, it was only natural that she be given responsibility for the oncology division. Her job included daily meetings with oncologists, interviews with patients who used the drugs her company sold, and a review of the vast medical research on the subject. In her job, Lyndsey came into contact with hundreds of terminally ill and long-term care patients, and their situation sometimes made Lindsey herself feel physically ill.

Lyndsey's **Malignant NAF** continued to warn her – morning, noon, and night – to stay on the alert, to learn as much as possible about cancer and not stick her head in the sand.

From time to time, Lyndsey took a pleasant walk through the maternity ward of the hospitals she visited. Then, suddenly, her NAF popped up to remind her that everything was temporary, that in the end all these babies would end up in the oncology unit.

By the time Lyndsey came to my workshop she was mentally exhausted. After hearing her story, I realized that she must make an immediate and drastic change in her environment.

The many long hours she invested in her job drained her of every last drop of positive energy, leaving her exposed to **Malignant NAF** and its threats.

The first change Lyndsey decided to make was to change her place of work – her physical environment. First, she requested a transfer from the oncology unit to the maternity ward. She was fascinated by this new field. She began to read professional literature on the subject and met happy mothers with their newborns.

Lyndsey also defined a new boundary for her parents and asked them to stop updating her about their friends who were ill. **Malignant NAF** still tried his luck now and again, reminding her to keep abreast of developments in oncology. But Lyndsey, encouraged by the change she'd made in her environment, decided to define a conceptual boundary and not read a single article about cancer for at least one year. She found plenty of other interesting things to fill her reading time, such as thrillers and romance novels. She stopped limiting her TV watching to the Science Channel. Gradually, she felt **Malignant NAF** losing its power and influence. Lyndsey became stronger, and, within a year of making these changes, she realized that she no longer felt the obsessive need to torture herself with information that made her life miserable. Lyndsey finally started living!

2. Get Rid of Your "Energy Drainers"

The second thing we must do to shape our environment so that it pulls us up and supports us on the way is to rid ourselves of our "energy drainers."

What is an "Energy Drainer"?

Energy Drainers are all those little things that disturb and trouble us but which we learn to tolerate in the course of our lives. We have the capacity to change them or rid ourselves of them, but we don't. All this unfinished business in our lives drains us of tremendous amounts of energy. And since we do nothing to change the situation, these things continue to bother us and squeeze out every last drop of our remaining energy, which causes us to project negative vibes and attract the things we don't want into our lives.

- How many times have we decided that today is the day to sort out all of our paperwork and organize our desk, but the whole day goes by without our completing the task? It's true. We had a thousand more important things to do, but we still cringe in frustration every time we pass our desk and see the terrible mess there. (Energy drainer in the physical environment)

- How many times have we decided to fix a broken electrical appliance, only to find that as the days go by we begin managing without it and adjusting to the less favorable living conditions? (Energy drainer in the physical environment)

- How many times have we decided to end an unhealthy relationship with a friend but are unable to do so for nostalgic reasons? (Energy drainer in the human environment)

- How many times have we preferred to delay an unpleasant or difficult conversation but instead found that the situation became worse and continued to trouble us? (Energy drainer in the human environment)

- How many times have we watched a TV program that not only did nothing to benefit us but ended up making us feel worse? (Energy drainer in the conceptual environment)

If we compare our bodies to an energy supply, our environment is capable of either replenishing that supply or depleting it. Our energy supply accompanies us on our journey through life, in our quest to fulfill our Inner Core. We must ensure that it never runs out. The energy drainers in our environment gradually diminish our supply of energy. In the long run, we find ourselves expending vast amounts of energy on things that disturb us and are unable to transfer positive energy to the really important things.

As human beings, we tend to come to terms with things. But when these are disturbing or destructive things, not coming to terms with them prevents us from choosing to live the lives we desire and attracting what is truly important to us. We pay a very dear price for our inaction: discomfort, wasted energy, anxiety, depression - all fertile ground for NAFs that we could have avoided.

Considering all of the other things we could be doing if we were rid of all these disturbances, we're actually paying double.

If we decide to take the initiative to see to all our unfinished business and rid ourselves of all different types of energy drainers, we'll be filled with positive energy; we will no longer feel we're wasting our time, and, most importantly, we'll feel like an enormous weight has been lifted from our shoulders. Warning: Even if we manage to clear our energy drainers from our lives, our NAFs will always be there, lying in wait. **Pressure NAF** will urge us to get everything done at once in order to keep functioning. **Worthless NAF** will blame us for not getting rid of our energy drainers sooner. Well, I've got some friendly advice for you. Okay, you decided to take care of your unfinished business and rid yourself of your energy drainers. Fine. But don't blame yourself for not doing it sooner. Better late than never. Do everything at your own pace, according to your schedule and convenience. If you pressure yourself, you'll never achieve your goal.

Sophie lived with her husband in a rented apartment. Every time she entered the apartment, Sophie experienced strange sensations of alienation, coldness, and depression. Although it suited them in terms of size and rent, it was very dark and gloomy. Sophie had never before realized that the most important thing in a home was brightness and airiness. The thing she loved best about her previous apartment was the way the sunlight streamed in through the windows during the whole day. She loved to bask in its enveloping warmth as she sat on the sofa reading the newspaper. But in this new apartment, despite its excellent location and appropriate size, she felt she didn't belong. To compound the dark, depressing atmosphere, the entire living room was painted green. Yes, that's right – a dark brownish green. Sophie detested the color and quickly noticed that she began to spend less and less time in her new home. She would go in and out as quickly as possible without lingering to enjoy "being at home."

One Saturday morning, Sophie awoke to find her husband in the living room, dressed in old jeans and a work-shirt. He had a paintbrush in his hand and was surrounded by buckets of white paint. He told her he was sick and tired of living in such a gloomy place and that he was painting the living room white. At first Sophie was angry. Since it was not their home but a rented apartment, why should they waste their time and money painting someone else's property? Besides, she told him, nothing could possibly change the way she felt about the apartment. Sophie's husband told her he'd had enough and wasn't prepared to sit in a green living room any more. The cost of the paint was minimal, and he was willing to invest the time and effort needed to brighten up their home. Finally, he managed to convince Sophie, who picked up a paintbrush and started to help him.

A few hours later, Sophie stood in her bright white living room and even managed a small satisfied smile. She couldn't believe how such a small change could completely change her feelings about her home. Rejuvenated, Sophie began to plan where to hang all the pictures they'd brought from their former home. Sophie, or rather her husband, was not prepared to accept the things that bothered him in his environment, and he took positive action. It was so simple, so very simple, to get rid of their energy drainer. It was what finally helped them feel at home in their new apartment.

The moral of the story: Even if the source of the disturbance is temporary, even if it does not belong to us but is something we use or live in, even if it means investing a little extra effort, it is worth every penny, and every NAF.

Action Steps- Take the Initiative and Get Rid of Your Energy Drainers

Under each "environment" heading, note three things that disturb you and drain your energy:

Human Environment:

1. _____

2. _____

3. _____

Physical Environment:

1. _____

2. _____

3. _____

Conceptual Environment:

1. _____

2. _____

3. _____

Now select one energy drainer from each category and start to work on it:

Human Environment		
Energy Drainer	*Action Required*	*When?*

Physical Environment		
Energy Drainer	*Action Required*	*When?*

Conceptual Environment		
Energy Drainer	*Action Required*	*When?*

3. Surround yourself with "Energy Snacks"

The third step to take for constructing a more supportive environment is to surround ourselves with "Energy Snacks."

Like any high protein snack, our energy snacks are small but concentrated and provide our bodies with a "stimulant injection" of energy.

What sorts of energy snacks should we surround ourselves with?

They can be found everywhere – in our conceptual, physical, and human environments. We just need to be able to identify them and reach out to grab them.

Energy Snacks in the Human Environment:

If we surround ourselves with people whose company is pleasant, who do not make us feel pressured or threatened, we have surrounded ourselves with energy snacks.

If we want to embark on a new project and find a friend who is also interested, and then we proceed to work together and encourage each other, we have surrounded ourselves with another energy snack.

Energy Snacks in the Physical Environment:

If we treat ourselves to the vacation we've always dreamed of, or just have an enjoyable weekend (with or without our partner), we have surrounded ourselves with another energy snack.

If we attend an exercise class, go to a fine restaurant, or partake in any other "treat" that makes us feel good, we have surrounded ourselves with another energy snack.

If we bring home a fragrant bouquet of flowers, hang a new picture on the wall, or do anything else that brightens up our private palace, we have surrounded ourselves with another energy snack.

Energy Snacks in the Conceptual Environment:

If we finally register to study something that has always interested us but that until now we have deferred for a thousand-and-one reasons, we have surrounded ourselves with another energy snack.

If we treat ourselves to a play or movie, or simply read a good book, we have surrounded ourselves with an energy snack. It might seem that we are already doing all these things. But the following exercise shows us (by helping us identify which has the greater influence – energy drainers or energy snacks), our energy "diet" is not always balanced. We will discover that it's the energy drainers that control our time, leaving us little chance to fill up on the energy snacks.

Action Steps – Identify the Energy Drainers and Energy Snacks in your Human Environment

Over the course of the coming week, pay careful attention to each person you come into contact with (friends, family, colleagues, etc). Think carefully about the effect each person has on you, and how he or she makes you feel.

Do you feel excited, alert, and energized in their company, or do they make you feel drained, tense, and introverted?

This is the best way to discover who drains your energy and who revitalizes you and gives you new energy.

Remember: your objective is to surround yourself increasingly with energy snacks, (which project positive vibes) and not energy drainers (which do the opposite).

And now, as promised, my tips for Code No. 5 – "Your Environment"

Tip 1 – Wean Yourself from Your Daily Diet of News

Have you ever stopped to consider the crazy reality we live in? Every day brings a new scandal, a new tragedy, a new political debacle. People are murdered, wounded, hurt in traffic accidents. Bad news is endless.

Unfortunately the society we live in supplies news at an alarming rate:

There are news programs 24/7 on radio and television.

The newspapers are filled with articles and commentaries about terror attacks, natural disasters, crimes, disease, etc. Add to that the non-stop negative information available on the Internet.

In other words, bad news gets high ratings. We become totally addicted to information and must have access to news 24 hours a day. We must know what is going on, must be up to date on what's happening, all the time!

But what does this do to us? How does it affect our mood, our energy levels, our motivation, and the vibes we project?

Are you aware of the negative effect of the excessive consumption of negative and stressful information on our lives?

I'm not suggesting that from this day forth you shut your eyes and ears and live in a euphoric bubble into which the news does not penetrate. But I do suggest you try to "wean" yourself from your heavy diet of news.

Try and set a limit to update yourself on the news just once a day. You can watch or listen to one major newscast per day – and that's it. No cheating! I promise you that whatever you need to know you'll find out from that newscast, and you won't feel "out of things." You'll find yourself getting up in the morning with a new glint in your eye and even a smile on your face. And, of course, you'll suddenly have an endless supply of free time on your hands!

Tip 2 – Let Your Environment Inspire You

Once you are able to recognize your Inner Core, and you know what you have to do to fulfill it, your environment can become a fertile source of inspiration. Make a conscious decision to open your eyes, prick up your ears, and look for little snippets of inspiration hiding in the world around you.

A fascinating article in the newspaper might fill your head with new and interesting ideas, ideas that could help you achieve your goals. Meeting an interesting person could open a new door to an unexpected place. Even an engaging TV program could have the same effect.

You have to decide that you are going to concentrate on finding "little sources of inspiration" in everything that surrounds you. You'll be surprised to see that they're everywhere!

Tip 3 – A New and Original Way to Tackle Your Chores

We are all human, and we all have commitments as well as rights. Even though the name of the game is to fulfill our Inner Core, there is no getting away from the daily chores and commitments that make up the bulk of our lives as working women, mothers, and homemakers. Of course we all have tasks we'd prefer to ignore, but we cannot afford that luxury. So how can we derive inspiration from our environment to help us with our daily tasks? This is where imagination and creativity come into play. Here are several helpful ideas for women like us, and you are most welcome to add your own.

- Make an elaborate promise. The pressure to keep your promise will ensure that you do what you've undertaken to do. For example: promise yourself that within a month you will lose ten pounds, and then tell all your friends. Their expectations will spur you on to keep your promise.

- If the house is a complete mess and you keep finding reasons not to tidy up, one good solution is to invite guests over. Then you have no choice - you have to knuckle down and start cleaning!

- If you have to present a project at work but are "unable" to start working on it, schedule a meeting with your boss for a week from today to bring him up to date on your progress, and show him your results. Now you have to start working on that project if you want to have something to show him!

- If you keep giving in to your lethargy and skipping your regular exercise sessions, make a standing arrangement with a friend to go to an exercise class or take a daily walk. You will think twice about canceling your arrangement and letting your friend down, and that way you're sure to get the regular exercise you need!

P.S. Now that you've cracked Code No. 5 - Your Environment, don't forget to open the accompanying workbook to on the fifth chapter and pamper yourself with some more "attractive" exercises!

CHAPTER 6

CRACKING CODE NO. 6 – SPRING INTO ACTION

"The future is not a result of choices among paths offered by the present, but a place that is created - created first in the mind and will, created next in activity."

— JOHN SCHAAR

So, what can we expect by cracking the sixth Code of the Law of Attraction – "Spring into Action?"

We'll understand the meaning of action, and learn what prevents us from taking action and applying the Law of Attraction in our lives. We'll learn how important it is to break down the barriers and simply start to act, despite our NAFs. We'll get action steps and tips on how to take action, break old habits, and celebrate our activity.

What is Action?

- I'll start that diet tomorrow.

- This is the week I'll ask about that promotion at work.

- That's it! I've had enough! I'm going to put her in her place, once and for all!

Do those statements sound familiar? We all make promises to ourselves about "later," but in practice these promises stay on the drawing board. They're never translated into concrete action.

So what is action, and how will it help us overcome the frenzy of our NAFs and attract what is truly important into our lives?

Action is anything that brings us closer to fulfilling the elements of our Inner Core.

We can compare our Inner Core to a seed. If we water it, fertilize it, and give it adequate sunlight, it will eventually sprout.

Our Inner Core elements will not sprout on their own. There's a lot of hard work involved. If we want to make good things happen to us, we have to make sure our lives are on the right track.

Here's a little story to illustrate this point: An elderly man prayed to God every day: "God, please make me win the lottery!" This went on day after day and month after month until one day St. Peter, who was sitting next to God, said, "You know, God, he seems like a good and pious man. Can't you just grant his wish and make him win the lottery? It's so important to him." God looked at St. Peter and smiled: "Peter, I would like nothing better than to help him win the lottery, but how can he win if he doesn't even buy a ticket?"

How can we expect to attract good things and make them happen if we don't do the legwork? How can we contend with our **"I am Worthless" NAF**, if we don't make an effort to increase our self-esteem?

How can we contend with our **Careeristus NAF** if we continue putting up with a depressing or demeaning job?

Action is what allows us to move forward, to feel better about ourselves. Just thinking positive thoughts isn't enough to create the reality we desire and attract the right types of opportunities. We also need to act. Action can mean taking the initiative, effecting change in our life, studying, being assertive, or even enjoying an outing with friends. The main thing is to be active, not passive. Action enables us to take responsibility for our lives and to proceed, one step at a time, towards attracting what is really important to us.

<u>Diana's Story</u>

Diana was always "one of the gang" – cheerful, friendly, and smart. She met Jack when she was in her early twenties and fell madly and passionately in love. She thought about Jack morning, noon, and night. He occupied her every waking (and non-waking) thought! Nothing mattered to her apart from Jack. Exactly one year after their first date, Jack broke up with Diana. He said that her obsessive love choked him, and that he just didn't feel the same about her. Needless to say, Diana took the breakup very badly. She never left the house and concentrated only on her studies. Her life was reduced to going to classes at the university, studying for tests, and watching TV in her spare time.

She became totally passive about anything connected with her social life, and she made no effort to find a new boyfriend. The disappointment she'd experienced, and the fear that it would happen again, prevented her from taking the initiative. It also prevented her from meeting and dating new men.

Years went by. By the time I met Diana she was in her late 40s, single with no children, living alone in her parents' house and serving as a model aunt to her sister's children.

Diana's story is a painful illustration of the dangers of behaving passively. A good-natured and intelligent woman like Diana missed out on her chance to find a life partner, become a mother, and build a home and family just because she remained a slave to unrequited love from years gone by.

Of course the pain was great, and hard to bear. But if, over the years, Diana would have just taken the initiative and joined a singles club, gone out and met people, taken up a hobby, or even sought counseling to help her overcome her problem, she might have stopped crying about the bitterness of her fate and changed the types of vibes she was projecting. In time she might have greatly increased her chances of attracting another love by acting to make it happen. Then she'd have been able to look back on her romance with Jack as merely a brief fling.

Why Should We Take Action?

Most of us have been subjected to that traumatic experience known as a "blind date." We prepare, get dressed up, put on makeup, wait... And then, we open the door to find ... the ultimate disappointment! The guy is not our type (to put it mildly) and we don't know how to handle the situation. "Just as long as nobody sees us ..." "Just let this nightmare end, and let me get back home." Then we make the inevitable decision to never ever again be tempted to go on a blind date!

But look at it this way: If we're unattached and interested in a relationship, a blind date has a fifty-fifty chance of succeeding. It might be disappointing, but then again, the guy just might be "the right one." If we sit at home alone, in front of the TV, we have no chance of entering a new relationship.

And so, each time we take action and go out on a blind date – fraught as it is with tension, anticipation, and discomfort – we increase our chances of finding "Mr. Right!"

In his book, *Acquired Optimism*, the psychologist Martin Zeligman explains why depression attacks twice as many women as men. Based on his research, he believes that "When bad things happen – women think and men act." He says that women "chew the cud." They analyze what happened, what they did wrong, what caused what, etc., and this increases the risk of depression. Men, on the other hand, act. They go out to play ball, drink with their friends, or set their minds to solving the problem. (If they've lost their job, for example, they will immediately start looking for a new one.)

Activity is usually preferable to inactivity, even if it's only a small, hesitant step. Quite often, influenced by our NAF, we prefer to remain passive and not take initiatives. **Failure NAF** reminds us that we will never succeed, so there's no point in even starting to take action. **"I am Worthless" NAF** claims we won't even understand what action to take. But if we simply start taking action, we will silence our NAFs. If our present situation is bad for us, any action, however slight, can improve the way we feel.

The effects of our activity will be much greater than that small step we took. They will snowball and have greater impact the further they reach.

Sometimes, when we start to take action, a new and unexpected path opens up before us. Meeting new people and learning new things, extracting ourselves from our current situation and making progress, achieves results. By taking these actions, we project enthusiasm and curiosity, and eventually we attract success.

Joanne's Story

Joanne was always the pretty one! With her long cascading hair, perfect skin, and shapely body, she was the prettiest girl in class and in the group she hung out with. Joanne was always aware of her appearance, which was evident in the way she dressed and the self-confident aura she projected (and even preceded her when she entered the room).

Over the years, Joanne was always careful to take care of her looks, even after giving birth to three children. Working out helped keep her body in shape, and for the most part she was satisfied with her appearance and the impression she projected.

However, as she grew older Joanne began to feel strange about her appearance. Her skin wasn't as elastic as it once was, and every morning when she looked in the mirror **Wrinkly NAF** whispered, *"Hey, look! You've got a new line on your forehead! NO! Don't smile!*

That only accentuates the lines around your eyes. Maybe you should wear a scarf round your neck. It's starting to droop."

Joanne became obsessed with her changing appearance. Throughout the day, **Wrinkly NAF** egged her on to compare herself to every woman she saw on the street, pointing out to her that her skin was looser than theirs. It also reminded her that she looked much older than her age, more like her husband's mother than his wife. It woke her up in the middle of the night, warning her that smashing her face into the pillow would cause even more wrinkles. She quickly rolled over to lie on her back.

Joanne's self confidence plummeted, and she began to feel depressed. Finally, she decided to take action. Since her physical appearance was so important to her, and her entire personality shone through her face, Joanne started to think about plastic surgery. As she was checking out her options, her **Wrinkly NAF** popped up, saying: *"Don't you dare have a facelift - you'll look like a monster! Your expression will look artificial. Just look at other women you know who've had a facelift. You don't want to end up like them!"*

Hypochondriac NAF argues that *"It's like any other operation. They'll give you a general anesthetic. Are you sure you want to put yourself through something like that?"*

And, of course, **Money, Money, Money NAF** claimed, *"It will cost you a fortune, and then you'll probably want surgery on your breasts, which will cost even more, and that will be followed by liposuction, etc. It will never end. Your finances are so precarious right now. How can you justify spending money on such luxuries?"*

Joanne almost allowed herself to be sucked into the whirlwind the NAFs brewed up. But then she decided that she was so unhappy with the way she looked that she'd do anything necessary to improve the situation. Joanne decided to overcome her fear of the operation and its outcome and to take action to achieve her goal. She checked out the risks of the surgery, and she did some research to find the best surgeon in her area. She talked to women who'd had similar surgery and were satisfied with the results. She did everything possible to avoid any possible complications. Just starting to act - by doing background research and talking to people – strengthened her and weakened hcr NAFs. Joanne knew she was doing the right thing for herself, and that she would be strong enough to live with the consequences. Joanne decided to take action in order to attract the reality she truly desired.

So What Prevents us From Acting?

Three main factors prevent us from taking action and advancing toward our objectives.

- Our need to remain in our "comfort zone" (Don't worry, an explanation follows immediately).
- Our habits and the difficulty of breaking them
- Our fear of change and failure.

Let's learn about each of these factors in more detail:

1. We are comfortable in our comfort zone

What is the "comfort zone"?

The comfort zone consists of all those things that don't threaten or deter us – familiarity, routine, habits, behavior patterns, and a "place" we know well. We operate within a comfort zone that doesn't confront us with challenges. We stay there because we feel uneasy whenever we venture beyond it.

A brief portrait of life in the comfort zone:

- We're comfortable asking for help from family members but not from friends.
- We find it easy to drive in familiar places but get nervous in new locations.
- We feel more at ease giving than receiving.
- We keep the same hairstyle, wear the same style of clothes, and use the same makeup, because we like to stick with what's familiar to us.

Though our comfort zone is very cozy, it's also very limiting. How does it limit us? To realize what's in our Inner Core, we sometimes need to leave familiar territory and do something new and different. Remaining in our current zone may give us no opportunity to express the elements of our Inner Core and our personal values.

It doesn't sound that complicated, does it? But it's a mixed blessing. Who jumps up, with no advance warning, every time we dare to leave our comfort zone? Why, it's our NAF, of course!

Our NAF uses all of its power to fortify our comfort zone. To convince us to stay there, it reminds us of the disasters that loom should we ever try to leave. Our NAF believes that the longer we remain in familiar territory - with no surprises, changes, or uncertainty - the better off we'll be. If we're brave enough to venture out, it will use all its power to lure us back into our comfort zone.

We listen wholeheartedly to our NAF, and rather than taking initiative and being proactive in order to attract new opportunities to our lives, we remain passive in our comfort zone.

Kathy's Story

For fifteen years, Kathy worked at as an accountant at a large educational software firm. She was an expert at analyzing financial reports, drawing conclusions, and knowing how to achieve the best results for her firm.

Kathy had one secret that she never shared with any of her colleagues: she did not know how to operate a computer. She was too frightened to go near one and would never think of turning one on. Kathy's comfort zone was everything connected to manual calculation: sharpened pencils, a large sheaf of papers, and a small pocket calculator. The thought of "leaving" her comfort zone in the direction of technological advancement, computers, Internet, and spreadsheets paralyzed Kathy completely. She was scared to death of technology.

Her **Failure NAF** assured her that she'd never be able to navigate the secret world of computers. To begin with, she was way too old.

She'd once enrolled for a beginner's computer course but left when she saw she didn't understand a thing.

Her **"What Will They Say" NAF** told her never to reveal her secret to anyone. It said she'd be fired the minute word got out.

As the years passed, each new technological advance tormented Kathy. She realized she was losing the expertise she'd always had. Everyone at the firm (except Kathy) communicated by email, and all the reports were computerized. Kathy was under tremendous emotional pressure as she tried to figure out how to continue doing her job without a computer, and how to keep her secret at the same time.

She relied on the departmental secretary, who already had a full workload without the extra tasks Kathy started delegating to her. The secretary would input the data, produce the reports, and even answer the emails from Kathy's colleagues. Kathy became increasingly more dependent on the departmental secretary, shifting more work in her direction, and the secretary began showing signs of dissatisfaction.

"I am Worthless" NAF claimed that Kathy was unworthy of her job, that over the years she'd become a burden on the department, and that it wouldn't be long before she was replaced. Kathy believed her NAF. Though she loved her job very much, she decided to resign before she was fired.

Kathy listened to her NAFs and chose to stay in her comfort zone of computer illiteracy. Instead of doing something, taking action – such as hiring a private tutor and learning once and for all how to use a computer – Kathy allowed her **Failure NAF** to control her and steer her fate. Kathy was too scared to leave her comfort zone and take positive action. She also listened to her **"What Will They Say" NAF**, and, not wanting to damage her pride if anyone discovered her secret, she preferred resigning to admitting the simple truth: "I don't know how to use a computer. I would like to change that by taking a course and learning."

In the end, Kathy acted against her heart's desire. She ignored the elements of her Inner Core and decided to resign from her job (which she still loved) and keep her secret safe. She relinquished the opportunity to attract the reality that she truly desired.

Action Steps – Recognize Your Comfort Zone

Choose one day, and "devote" it to recognizing your own comfort zones. For example:

What time do you wake up in the morning?

What, if anything, did you wear last night?

What is the "division of labor" at home in the morning? Who walks the dog? Who hurries the kids up? Who makes the coffee?

What clothing do you wear during the day?

Do you wear make up?

Do you travel the same route every day?

What do you say when you walk into the office?

How do you speak and behave with your coworkers? How do you speak and behave with your managers?

Why do I call these things the "comfort zones?"

Try to imagine what would happen if you decided to get up an hour earlier in the morning, to allow yourself some time alone?

What would happen if you decided to wear a sexy negligee for bed, instead of an old tracksuit?

What would happen if, just once, you didn't supervise the children in the morning and let them take responsibility for themselves?

What would happen if you went out without makeup? Or you wore a different style of clothing?

What would happen if you decided to stand up to your boss and put him in his place?

Does any of that sound difficult? Terrifying?

We know we're in our comfort zone when the very thought of leaving it frightens or paralyzes us. Our typical response is to shake our heads and find a good excuse for not taking action.

2. Break Old Habits? Never!

The second factor leading to inactivity is the difficulty we have breaking our habits.

Our habits have place of pride in our comfort zone. They play a dominant role in our decision to remain passive.

Try to think of a deep-rooted habit, one you can't even conceive of breaking. Is it that little something sweet that you "must have" after a meal? Is it that cigarette with your coffee? Or "your" side of the bed? Maybe it's your obsession with the news, which keeps you glued to the radio or TV.

Everyone has their own habits and behavior patterns that are hard, almost impossible, to change. But are they? Everything can be changed, especially behavior patterns resulting from habits, but only if we are determined and prepared to make an effort to change them.

Most of us don't initiate change because it's easy for us to remain in familiar territory. We tend to think that the familiar is the best thing for us. But how can we be sure of that if we never try anything else?

We believe we are incapable of changing our regular behavior patterns. But if we don't try, we'll never know.

At one of my workshops, Zoe, a teacher, told me that she was "addicted" to her afternoon nap. She would do anything to make sure she got that little sleep after lunch. Even at the university, she arranged her classes, even bumped some courses to the next semester, just to make sure she got the time for her afternoon nap. Several years later, when her children reached school age, Zoe realized that her afternoon nap had become an obsession and that it was coming at the expense of her children. They came home at lunchtime and needed help with their homework. While she was unable to give up her nap, she never did manage to get any sleep. Her **Kiddimus NAF** nagged her to get up immediately, that she was just wasting her time at the expense of quality time with her kids.

Zoe decided it was time to take action and change her habit – to forego her midweek afternoon nap. She wanted to spend more time with her children and be more involved in their lives. She would be so busy that she wouldn't have time to feel tired, and she would allow herself a real afternoon nap on the weekends. I met Zoe again a month after she made her decision. She told me that, amazingly enough, she had stuck to her new daily agenda and was able to accomplish much more than she ever believed possible. She was very pleased with her action but still didn't really believe that she had managed to break the habit of a lifetime.

Some habits are easy to break, and others are so deeply rooted within us that they are utterly resistant to change. We want to start initially with the habits that prevent us from doing what is really important to us.

Simply being aware that our habit controls us and making an attempt to change that situation are steps in the right direction.

Action Steps- Using the Law of Attraction to Break a Habit (Eating Chocolate)

Some of our most deep-seated habits can be broken by using the Law of Attraction. One example is the habit of eating chocolate to excess after a meal. Many chocoholics claim that no matter how many times they've thought about ending their habit, they couldn't make it through one single day without breaking open a chocolate bar.

When, , according to the Law of Attraction, we try to counter the habit with our actions, we're actually focusing on it to an even greater extent. We're more firmly entrenching it in our behavior, and our chances of doing away with it are dwindling. The solution, therefore, is to behave as if you've already overcome the problem. In other words, try to act in precisely the way you would like to see yourself act; perform the actions you want to attract into your life. If your desire is to end your insatiable demand for chocolate, act like someone who is not plagued with this desire. Take a look at people who can finish a meal without the craving for something sweet afterward, or who satisfy the urge by eating something sweet but healthy. Study their behavior. What mannerisms do they have? What do they do with their hands? You may discover, for example, that they prefer following up their meals with a steaming hot cup of coffee or exotic-flavored tea. The next time you have a craving for chocolate, try copying one of these mannerisms. Inside, you'll feel whatever it is the non-chocoholics feel. Eventually, you'll be less interested in the taste of that chocolate bar, and your habit will slowly fade away.

3. Failure and Change – How Terrifying!

The third factor causing our inactivity comes from two very stubborn NAFs that are committed to keeping us passive and convincing us that only bad things happen when we take action.

"I Don't Want to Change" NAF is responsible for our fear of any alteration in our routine, and our **Failure NAF** drills home the message that we'd better not do anything new because we're bound to fail.

"I Don't Want to Change" NAF repeats, like a broken record, that *"change only brings about trouble,"* and, of course, it makes us regret trying in the first place.

Our fear of change paralyzes us. Our NAF paints a terrible picture of the likely consequences of change, and we, of course, believe it.

But if the current situation is bad for us, change might improve it and open new doors for us, leading to new opportunities and a brighter future.

Even worse than the fear of change is the fear of failure. Our **Failure NAF** works overtime to convince us that "it's not worth starting" because we'll never succeed; we'll just be wasting our time, money, and energy.

Rita's Story

Rita had a reputation as an excellent baker. Her kitchen was always filled with the mouth-watering aroma of freshly baked rolls, cookies, and cakes. One day, Rita decided to turn her hobby into a business.

Even more than cooking and baking, Rita loved the reactions of her friends and family when they tasted her creations. She loved seeing the smile on their faces and the sparkle in their eyes when they bit into her tasty morsels, and she decided that she might as well make some money and enjoy herself at the same time.

Rita decided to open a home-based business and set up a small catering company for baked goods. She took the matter very seriously and began an enthusiastic marketing campaign. She chose a catchy name, printed business cards with her logo, and distributed spectacular flyers all over town. She became carried away in the euphoria of activity, initiative, creativity, and a lot of positive energy. Her name, and more importantly that of her baked goods, became a household word. Rita's enthusiasm, coupled with her activity, attracted many opportunities, and her business started booming within a short time.

The phone was soon ringing off the hook with orders for her Danish pastries, her melt-in-the-mouth cookies, and her specialty cakes. Rita was busy right from the start, and she knew she was on the right track.

One morning, the morning Rita will never forget, there was a knock at her kitchen door. Rita was in the middle of a large order of cakes, and her kitchen was in total disarray. There were two officials from the Health Department at the door. They had heard that she was operating a catering business from her home, and they were coming to inspect her kitchen. After the inspection, they explained to Rita that she could not continue to operate her business from her home because her kitchen did not meet Health Department standards. To keep operating her business, she would need to rent a commercial facility that meets departmental standards.

As Rita listened to them, she turned pale. She knew this was the end of her dream. She politely thanked her visitors, closed the door, sat down, and cried. At that moment, Rita gave up and did not try to find another solution. She invented all sorts of excuses and reasons for not renting an industrial facility, and, having convinced herself, she closed her business. She was scared off by the first obstacle in her path, and she allowed it to slam the door on her dream.

Even though our **Failure NAF** will try its best to convince us that it's not worth starting something, or that we should immediately stop what we've just started, I suggest the opposite.

You should start, try, continue, and take action. Those who never try make no mistakes. Or, as the old adage goes: If there are no obstacles in your path, you'd better check to make sure the road you're traveling on actually leads somewhere.

Failure is not something to fear. Failure is unavoidable. I, who have experienced and learned from failure, recommend that you try to make good on your own failures. In other words, as the saying goes, "When life gives you lemons, make lemonade."

How to cope with failure?

How do we do that? It's very simple. There are a few rules of thumb that help me and the women I coach to cope with failure and continue on with our lives:

1. View failure as a challenge on the way to success. First and foremost, you must never think of failure as the end of the world. You have to regard failure as a temporary setback, a fleeting episode, or an obstacle on the path success and realization of our Inner Core.

2. The second way to cope with failure is to use it as a tool for learning lessons and drawing conclusions. Failure should be regarded as a lesson in life. Failures, problems, and obstacles are life's encyclopedia. We must understand what we did wrong, where we made mistakes, and how we might have solved the problem differently. We should avoid asking ourselves, "Why me?" because we are only demonstrating victimhood and self-pity, showing how judgmental and miserable we are. What we need to ask is, "What can I learn from this?"

3. The third way to cope with failure is to ask yourself, "What's the worst case scenario?": Every time **Failure NAF** starts drilling our brains with its convincing arguments, or each time we do, indeed, experience failure, we've got to project the "worst case scenario" in our minds. What, after all, is the worst that could happen? Sit in a comfortable chair and let your imagination run wild. Go through one undesirable scenario after another until you're sure you thought of the worst. If you act in a particular way, what will people say? How will you answer them? What will happen next? Keep

going until you come up with ways of dealing with the consequences. What happens when you start responding?

In this way, you'll understand exactly what you're afraid of, and you'll know how to combat those fears. You may realize, after envisioning the entire awful scenario in your mind, that the fear wasn't so great after all and that you've inflated it out of proportion. Most importantly, you'll discover that you're able to deal with it. I'm quite sure you'll see that the mountain was a molehill after all.

4. The fourth way to cope with failure is to keep the statistics in mind: Research has demonstrated that behind many a success there are at least three or four major failures. What distinguishes people who have realized themselves, discovered what's in their Inner Core, and experienced success in life is the simple fact that they didn't throw up their hands in despair the first time they failed. They continued to pursue their dreams and not give in to self-pity. As every experienced salesperson can testify, it's usually only after the tenth sales pitch that results begin to show. The loser is the first person to throw in the towel.

5. The fifth way to cope with failure is to take a somewhat different approach if you are experiencing serial failures: As Nietzsche once commented, tongue in cheek, it's only a madman who repeats the same action over and over again and expects different results. I recommend that you rethink your actions. Perhaps your multiple failures are a sign that you need to be taking a new direction, trying a more creative approach. The doors that open up before you will lead the way to a better future! You'll read more about this in another few pages, under the heading "The Art Of Letting Go."

My First Failure at the Women's Mornings Center

Just as I'll never forget that sweet taste of my first kiss, I'll never forget the bitterness of my first failure at the "Women's Mornings" Center.

From the minute I decided to set up my Cultural Center for Women, I knew that it had to be really special – different from other centers of its type. Apart from the uniquely designed sessions I'd be teaching and coaching, I wanted to offer a relaxing atmosphere – something out of the ordinary. I looked for a place that would suit my (meager) budget but would still be attractive. Eventually, after weeks of hard work, I found the spot – a nature center. Though located in the middle of a residential suburb, the site was surrounded by trees and overlooked a gorgeous lake complete with swans. As soon as I arrived, I entered a new world. It was so picturesque, with benches overlooking the lake, birds singing in the trees, classrooms with enormous windows overlooking the amazing view, and even secluded spots to hold sessions outdoors. Yes, there were even "classrooms" outside, in the middle of the woods, with benches carved from tree trunks and a small stump in the center that served as the trainer's desk.

As soon as I saw it, I knew this was the place for me. I knew it was the setting I wanted as a base for my activities. It would attract many women, and, more importantly, the message I wanted to convey in my courses would have even greater impact in this picturesque, relaxing setting. I spoke with the owner of the place, reached an agreement, and closed the deal. I decided it was important to accentuate the natural advantage of my location, and I devised the slogan: "A Pocket of Nature in the Heart of the City – culture, coaching, enrichment and fun!"

In all of my advertising, I stressed the message of the spectacular view, calmness, and tranquility. I knew this would be the ideal place for me to conduct my regular activities and, even more so, to hold my opening event.

I spent many months planning the opening. I took care of every little detail, selecting a team of professional lecturers and trainers, compiling a list of potential clients, preparing flyers and distributing them in every possible location, advertising in the local papers, arranging for media coverage, and preparing an attractive opening presentation. I ordered appetizing and attractive refreshments, took care of parking arrangements, hired valets, prepared signposts, invited a celebrity to kick off the event, and even hired on-site babysitters to free young mothers who came with small children and give them a break from their regular routine.

I planned the event down to the last second. It goes without saying that I was too excited to sleep the night before. Pumped up with adrenalin, I arrived early at the location to take care of last minute arrangements.

Then the guests started to arrive – women, more women, and still more women. Young women, older women, ladies of leisure, businesswomen, company directors and salaried employees, women with children and women without. I greeted them all at the entrance and was elated by the turnout for my opening event. Everyone was enchanted by the beautiful surroundings and the description of my unique courses. They wondered how I'd found such a perfect location – a "pocket of nature" in the middle of the city.

The opening event went as planned, and many women registered for my workshops, coaching sessions, and courses.

You must be wondering where the failure comes into the story. Be patient, I'm getting there…

At the end of one of the most successful days of my life, I was euphoric. My dream had come true. My vision was beginning to become a reality. I'd attracted what I really wanted. It was unbelievable!

The following day, I scheduled a meeting with the owner of the location to update her on the number of classrooms I wanted to rent, given the large number of registrants. As soon as I saw her, I realized that something in her demeanor had changed.

She received me very coldly and said she had something to tell me. Scowling, she explained that she hadn't expected such a large turnout for the opening and never imagined so many people would register for the courses. She said she would not be able to accommodate us. The place was just not built for so many people, and I'd need to find an alternative location.

As I listened to her, I stood rooted to the spot. Even though the agreement I'd signed with her covered only the opening event, and I'd agreed I would sign a separate contract for the classrooms once I knew how many I needed, I had verbally agreed with her on the days of the week and the exact dates and hours that I'd be using the facility. I was stunned. It's hard to describe the extent of my anger, disappointment, frustration, and stress. My NAFs went into overdrive. Of course, **Failure NAF** said *"That's it! It's all over now! There is no way you'll find another location, let alone one as beautiful and picturesque as this. You might as well close the center now, in fact, the sooner the better, before you cause yourself any further embarrassment."*

Pressure NAF warned that *"there's no chance you'll find what you're looking for on such short notice! After you built up their expectations, everyone will be disappointed by another location, and no-one will turn up for your activities."* **"What Will They Say?"** NAF chipped in: *"Just think about those women! As soon as they hear that after just one meeting you've changed the location, they won't take you seriously. You'll get a reputation as an amateur."*

"What Have I Done to Deserve This?" NAF added fuel to the fire: *"How could she do such a thing to you? Where is her sense of commitment? Why has this happened after all your hard work?"*

And, last but not least, **Money, Money, Money NAF** reminded me, *"Just think how much this is going to cost you! Where will you find the money? Now you have to change all your business cards, all the catalogs you prepared. Everything will have to be changed because it all contains the wrong address. And you still haven't worked out how much a new place will cost."*

However, despite this very unpleasant experience, I knew I had to pull myself together and take immediate action. The courses would be starting in exactly one week, and I needed a place to conduct them. Otherwise, my entire vision would bite the dust.

I started to invest all my energy into finding alternative locations with a large number of classrooms to accommodate so many women. I told all my friends about my search, and luckily one of them, a leading figure in the local community, suggested an alternative location at nominal rent. The place wasn't as picturesque and beautiful as the nature center, and the windows didn't overlook a swan-studded lake or a forest. But the classrooms were spacious, the building was centrally located, the rent was even more reasonable, and, most importantly, the people I'd be doing business with were trustworthy.

I decided to sign an agreement, and, in hindsight, this turned out to be my best move. I was dealing with charming people, key figures in the local community who respected my activities, brought even more women to the center, and generally cooperated with me every step of the way. To break the news to the participants, I convinced the owner of the nature center to allow me to hold the next meeting there, and then, after everyone arrived, I explained that, unfortunately, I was unable to continue the courses in that location. They were all very disappointed, but when I explained the circumstances, they forgot their anger, sympathized with me, and promised they would come to my new location. They said that even though the nature center was charming and very special, the most important consideration for them was the content of the courses and workshops – not the surroundings.

And so I survived my first failure, which I can now look back on and regard as just another obstacle on the road to success.

So, how do you start to act in order to attract what you want?

I suggest four methods to help us overcome passivity and start taking initiatives:

1. Step out of your comfort zone .
2. Just start!
3. Practice the Art Of Letting Go (when you need to).
4. Celebrate being active.

1. Step out of your comfort zone

Why should we step out of our comfort zone?

Each of us has her own comfort zone, and if we stay in it forever we'll never practice taking risks, never face up to our fears and contend with the unknown. But, more significantly, we'll never take the initiative to change and to attract something better for ourselves.

Each time we try to leave the boundaries of our comfort zone (in spite of our NAF), or each time we change our habits and break free from our familiar behavior patterns, we move one step closer to a sense of empowerment. We feel strengthened and have renewed our self-confidence to continue. We'll be able to leave that comfort zone more often, in all sorts of challenging situations.

Leaving our comfort zone is a major blow to our NAF, which understands we no longer need its protection. As we move further outside our comfort zone, and the influence of our NAFs grows weaker, we will have a wider selection of behaviors at our disposal and greater freedom to decide what we really want to attract into our lives and what kind of reality we desire.

Action Steps- Step Out of Your Comfort Zone

Begin by leaving the confines of your comfort zone for minor, everyday things. That way, by the time you're ready to realize the values of your Inner Core and take action, it will be much easier for you to leave the comfort zone at more challenging times.

Over the course of the next week, choose something new each day that signifies a step outside your comfort zone - even if the current situation seems preferable. For example:

Decide to change your hairstyle.

Wear clothes that aren't your usual colors.

Allow your children free reign in something they'd like to do. Say "No!" just to see what will happen

Drive a different route to wherever you're going that day.

The idea is to practice leaving the safety of the comfort zone.

How did you feel the first time you made a change and left the comfort zone? How did you feel the second time, and the time after that? Was it so terribly difficult?

Liza's Story

Liza knew that when she married her husband, David, she was, essentially, marrying his entire family. She had no way of knowing how true that cliché would be in her case. David's mother had always tended to compare Liza's "performance" to that of her daughter, David's sister: the way she disciplined her children, her housekeeping, her relationship with her husband, etc.

On every single visit, Liza's mother-in-law made a point of saying what a shame it was that Liza didn't prepare David's favorite meals for him. And how thin and pale he looked. And how sad it was that Liza didn't invest more time and energy in the children. How was it possible that David's sister's daughter could already read and write, but Liza's daughter couldn't even recognize the letters of her own name?

For Liza, each visit was a nightmare, and afterwards she was attacked by a swarm of NAFs. **Kiddimus NAF** accused her of not being a good mother. **Please Everybody NAF** told her she should try to please her mother-in-law and invite her over more, prepare David's favorite meal, make sure the house was immaculate, and so on. Liza preferred to avoid confronting her mother-in-law and expressing her true feelings. She found every visit totally frustrating.

The last straw, which brought about a turning point in Liza's attitude, came when David's father died. David's mother approached him and asked if she could come and live with him and his family in their apartment. She was all alone, terribly miserable and helpless, and the obvious option would be for her to come and live with her dear son and his family, who would surely welcome her with open arms. Her son didn't respond immediately, but told her he needed to discuss the matter with his wife.

When he did, Liza felt as if her entire world was caving in on her. How could she possibly live with that woman, someone who made her life so miserable and caused her to feel worthless? But, just then, her **Please Everybody NAF** started working overtime and told her, *"You don't abandon people in their hour of need."* She couldn't just desert her husband's mother like that. She was newly widowed and needed their help right now. Liza knew that if her mother-in-law came to live in their home, it would cause tension that could lead to the break-up of the family she'd worked so hard to create and preserve. She was certain that having his mother around constantly would place her husband in an impossible position, and she and David would eventually start arguing, and who knows where it might end.

Liza decided to take the bull by the horns – to step out of her comfort zone and, just once, to stand up for herself. She wasn't aiming to please everyone else but to do what she thought was best for herself and her family. Liza told her husband that she didn't want his mother to come and live with them. She was prepared to help her in any other way possible. But bringing her into their home was too much and could end up destroying their own family. David understood how his wife felt, and Liza thought – for the first time in her relationship with her mother-in-law – that she had done the right thing. She had stepped out of her comfort zone, said *"No!,"* attracted what she really wanted, and felt wonderful afterwards.

Identify what you're gaining and what you're losing by staying within your comfort zone (and, at the same time, even lose some weight...)

We are comfortable in our comfort zone!

We're not willing to let go of it. Each time we try to leave the boundaries of our comfort zone, it's hard for us to do it, even hard to decide to take that first step. The reason is so simple. We've also got some gains by staying there. Until we recognize these gains and weigh them against the losses brought by the very same comfort zone, we won't be able to take that first step and prepare ourselves for the task. What do I mean? In one of my workshops, while I was explaining the idea of the comfort zone and the importance of locating it and then stepping out of it, one women suddenly said, "I know what my comfort zone is… My comfort zone is – food and fat! I feel comfortable when I eat, and when I keep on eating."

"And so," I asked her, "What are you losing by staying in that comfort zone?"

"Oh," she answered. "I'm getting fatter, pound by pound, and I'm ruining both my health and my appearance."

"In other words," I said, "the loss is clear to you. So why do you keep overeating? There must be some gain hidden there - besides the gain in weight. Try finding that gain that's hiding in your comfort zone."

"The gain," she responded, "is the compensation and comfort I get from the food. I feel good when I eat. It relaxes me and pampers me."

"And I'm telling you there's some other gain hiding there, deeper inside. And if you don't find it, it's going to be very hard for you to cut down on what you eat."

The woman went home with my "assignment" still ahead of her. She promised she'd think about it before the next workshop. When that day came, she entered the room excitedly: "I discovered the real gain hiding behind all those pounds of fat. I know why I've been steadily gaining weight for the past five years. I believe that if I'm fat, I can avoid having sex very often with my husband. If I'm physically repulsive, he won't be attracted to me, and he won't demand sex all the time. Our marriage has reached a status quo we can live with. The fact is that I'm no longer interested in sex very much at this point."

"Now we're talking," I told her. "In coaching jargon, that's what we call a 'pivotal moment.' It's the point when the process changes direction. Now you see what's really hiding there deep inside your comfort zone. You've identified the gain, and now you can balance it against the loss, decide what your next steps will be, and begin to act in a way that attracts into your life - finally - the reality you truly want."

"Let me fill you in on something else," I continued. Behind that gain there's another thing hiding - a belief that is restricting you to a very great extent. 'If I'm thin, I'll need to have sex with my husband more often.' You are the only one who decided to grant legitimacy to this restricting belief. To leave your comfort zone, you'll first need to bid farewell to that belief! If you and your husband have reached a status quo in which you're both satisfied with your marriage, you probably don't need to be sexually intimate any more than you are right now. No one can dictate to you how often to have sex. You need to understand and believe that you, only you, dictate the frequency, regardless of whether you're fat or thin. Only then can you bid farewell to your comfort zone and to those excess pounds as well.

Action Steps – Increase the Readings on Your Valuemeter

Now that you've started acting by stepping out of your comfort zone, the time has come to move on - to leave the real comfort zone and proceed with realizing your personal values.

Choose a value that you regard as important but which received a relatively low rating on your Valuemeter (Chapter 2). Decide what you want to do to make this value a prominent part of your life. Write down three definitive steps you will take to give this value a higher reading on our Valuemeter.

The personal value I want to promote is:

_____

What I have to do to make this value more prominent in my life:

1 _____

_____

2 _____

_____

3 _____

_____

Remember, so far in your life you haven't given much priority to acting on these steps. When you decide to do so, your NAF will probably go crazy and come up with all sorts of arguments, but this time you are equipped with the skills to face it.

Marcia's Story

Marcia was always ambitious. She was bound for professional success and planned her career down to the last detail, even before she graduated, with honors, with a B.A. in Economics.

She knew that she wanted to start off as an account manager in a large advertising agency, climb her way up the ladder until she managed several accounts, and eventually open her own agency. Marcia's most important personal values were self-expression, independence, initiative, and excellence.

Marcia valued herself. She knew exactly what she was worth and how good she was in her field. She did, indeed, begin to work as an account manager at a large advertising firm in town. After three years, with several large and important accounts under her belt, she decided it was time to move on. She decided to look for a new job at a larger company, one that offered a higher salary, but, more importantly, better prospects for promotion. Marcia wanted to be a director. She told her boss she was leaving because she wanted a higher-level position. Her boss said he was very sorry but had no offer for her at the time. Marcia left her job and began an enthusiastic search for something better.

She was confident that advertising executives would want to snap up such an attractive candidate and that it wouldn't take long at all to find what she was looking for. Three months of intensive searching, however, brought no results, and Marcia began to lose her self-confidence. She combed the newspaper and online want ads endlessly, but found nothing. On the rare occasion that something looked even halfway promising, she'd send off her resume, but she didn't get a single reply.

Marcia's **Worthless NAF** soon found its way to her ear and ranted that it had been a mistake to leave her previous job. She wasn't such an attractive candidate, and the job market was flooded with many better candidates. From now on, it told her, she'd have to compromise if she wanted to get back into her field, because no manager would want to hire her after such a long period of unemployment. Marcia thought about it all the time. She regretted her actions, and **"I Told**

You So" NAF had a field day! Her **Failure NAF** claimed that it was pointless to check the want ads every day because there was never anything suitable; and even if there was, she had no chance of getting the job.

Marcia sat at home, feeling sorry for herself. One day she spotted an ad that jumped out at her. The largest advertising agency in the country was looking to hire a Senior Account Manager with at least three years' experience and a relevant academic education. When Marcia saw the ad, she felt butterflies in her stomach. She began to feel the excitement that had faded and thought that maybe she'd finally found what she was looking for. The ad touched Marcia's Inner Core and she knew, and felt in her body, that it would be a golden opportunity to fulfill the personal values that were so important to her.

Marcia sent off her resume and waited for the phone to ring. But it never did. Her **Failure NAF** popped up and told her, *"If they haven't called by now, they won't be calling."* It reminded her that there were hundreds of applicants for every position this attractive, and, *"Why do you think that they would choose you, after you've been sitting at home for months? Anyway, if they do call, don't get your hopes up. You have no chance of actually getting the job."* Marcia realized that the job was a once-in-a-lifetime opportunity, and she decided to take action – to step out of her comfort zone.

Marcia sent off her CV and followed up by calling the company's HR director to convince him that she was the best person for the position. Her **"What Will They Say?"** NAF sprang up and told her that the HR Director would think she was strange. She would appear desperate, tactless, and possibly even impertinent. In a momentary impulse, Marcia overcame all her fears, stepped out of her comfort zone, and called the agency, asking to speak to the HR director. Marcia introduced herself briefly and told him that she was calling about the job she'd applied for. The director said that the candidates were being screened, and that if she hadn't been contacted by now, it meant that she was not suitable for the position. Marcia took a deep breath and told him that she considered herself to be an ideal candidate for the position and that all that she wanted was fifteen minutes of his time. She told him that he had nothing to lose by allowing her to come for an interview. He'd have a chance to see for himself that she was telling the truth. If she were unsuitable, he'd have wasted a quarter hour of his time; but if indeed she was the most suitable candidate, it would be the best quarter hour he ever spent. The HR director was pleasantly surprised by Marcia's directness and decided to invite her for an interview. It goes without saying that during the interview Marcia projected enthusiasm, interest, confidence, and dedication. As a result, she attracted the outcome she desired – she got the job. Sometime later, her new boss told her that he was so impressed by her self-confidence, professionalism, creative thinking, and strong belief in herself that he "had no choice" but to offer her the job.

It would have been easier for Marcia to stay within the familiar boundaries of her characteristic behavior – to never pick up the phone and simply hope that the HR director would see fit to call her for an interview. But she placed her personal values at the top of her list of priorities, stepped out of her comfort zone, and did something that initially required a good deal of courage but afterward became less daunting. By leaving her comfort zone and projecting positive vibes, Marcia achieved her goal and took one step further toward fulfilling her Inner Core.

Action Steps- A Moment With Your NAF

When you read about how other women have gathered the courage and stepped out of their comfort zone, your NAF is probably jumping up and down, demanding to be heard. So, let's expose it.

Write down what your NAF is saying to you:

_____

_____

_____

What are your other voices saying?

_____

_____

_____

2. Just Start

The second method that helps us start to take action in order to attract what we want is expressed very well by those two words: "Just Start!"

"I don't know what I want to do. I just know for sure that I don't want things to continue as they are now."

"I have no idea where to begin" Does that sound familiar?

Most of us have no idea what our true direction is and what we have to do to fulfill our Inner Core. We know for sure that everything we've done up to now has led nowhere and done nothing to help us fulfill our Inner Core and our personal values. In fact, the opposite is true - our actions have merely buried our Inner Core deeper inside us, and meanwhile we're giving our NAF plenty of nourishment.

So how do we start?

It's very simple – we just start! Start something, anything. The direction will come later. We must follow our heart and heed what it tells us. A new direction will then open up before us. It may not be clear at first, but all will become clear in due course.

We all suffer from the *"here and now"* syndrome. We want to know everything, right now. We want to solve everything immediately. Uncertainty is the mother of all sin, and we can't bear anything "foggy." That is why we are afraid of change, especially long-term change. But, unfortunately, we don't have a magic wand, and things don't happen by themselves. Patience is the name of the game – we must learn to be patient.

Try and imagine the course of your life as though it were a jigsaw puzzle. Each day you add a new piece to complete the picture. If you put a piece in the wrong place but try to force it in anyway, the picture will look a bit distorted, and the piece will never really fit there. It takes time to complete the entire picture. But as the picture gradually begins to take shape, it gets easier to find the missing pieces.

We have to start with small steps and not be scared of the great mountain ahead of us. After the first small step comes another small step, and then another and another until we finally reach the top of the mountain.

Lauren's Story

Lauren worked as a preschool teacher for more than ten years. She loved children, totally and unquestionably. She loved listening to them and guiding them, and she had limitless patience for them. She'll never forget the day when the manager of the daycare center where she worked asked to speak to her. Lauren thought they would be discussing a new project idea and was stunned when, sitting opposite the woman she so respected and admired, she was told coldly and calmly that, due to budgetary constraints, her employment at the center would be terminated. No further explanation, no beating around the bush.

Lauren felt as though she'd been struck on the head with a hammer. She went home, totally agitated, and that's when her NAFs went to work. Her **"I am Worthless" NAF** popped up to tell her she probably deserved it, that she wasn't good enough.

Her **Money, Money, Money NAF** reminded her that they could not survive financially on her husband's salary alone. What would happen? They had just bought a new apartment and started renovating it. How would they manage? **"What Will They Say?" NAF** warned that she would never be able to look her friends in the eye again. How could she tell them that she, Lauren, the wonderful preschool teacher, had been fired? What would they think of her? What about her professional reputation? Her **Failure NAF** added that now she would have to sit at home, and she would never find a job. Who would hire a preschool teacher who'd been fired from her previous position?

Sadly, Lauren sought advice from a friend, who suggested that she try a yoga class. She told Lauren that yoga would make her feel calm, help her organize her thoughts and plan her future. Lauren signed up for a nearby yoga class, and was enchanted. The yoga helped her silence her NAFs, and every day she found herself eagerly awaiting the next lesson. Lauren thought that if she found yoga so fascinating, it might be worth learning everything she could about it. She started researching the subject, which led her to decide to study yoga professionally. And so she progressed, step by step, and found herself living her life more "for the moment" and concentrating less on "what might happen."

One day Lauren's friend asked her to look after her three-year-old son. Not wanting to miss her yoga class, Lauren was forced to take the little boy with her. During the lesson, the little boy became bored and asked Lauren if he could join in and do the exercises with her. Lauren hesitated but backed down in the end. Then, suddenly, like a bolt from the blue, it hit her! Lauren realized what she'd been looking for. She felt an intense excitement filling her body. She was elated. She knew exactly which direction to follow: she would set up her own business and teach yoga to kids. The combination of children and yoga was ideal for her. Lauren began acting by taking one small step – getting out of the house and joining the yoga class – without knowing where she would end up. And suddenly a whole new world of options opened up before her. She had only to choose the most suitable one for her. Lauren fulfilled her Inner Core.

Action Steps – Outline Your Goals and Activities for the Coming Year

1. My three goals for the coming year:

   Goal 1: _____

   _____

   Goal 2: _____

   _____

   Goal 3:_____

   _____

2. The first three actions I must take to realize my goals for the next month:

   1: _____

   _____

   2: _____

   _____

   3: _____

   _____

3. The first three actions I must take to realize my goals for the coming year:

   1: _____

   2: _____

   3: _____

Remember: Your goals must be challenging but attainable!

3. Practice the Art of Letting Go (when you need to)

"The most elementary, most external requirement for growth is the willingness to let go of what you believe should happen"

(A. H. Almaas)

This is the third method for starting to take action, but it's one that borders on questionable taste.

What do I mean?

Every one of us – or nearly every one – has an unborn baby inside, something we really, really long for and dream about. But, for some reason, we haven't yet achieved it. The second it arrives, it will make us overwhelmingly happy, but... nada, zip. It's not that we're not working for it; the fact is that we never stop working for it. Yet it refuses to come. The outcome we so long for never arrives.

So what happens? Gradually, we find ourselves spinning in a whirlpool of intense emotions, unnecessary stress, and obsession. Yes, obsession. And that obsession can drive us crazy. We can barely think about anything else. Everything revolves around our unfulfilled desire. It's that or nothing. If I don't have it, I suffer. Nothing else suffices. I'll come back to life only when I've achieved my dream.

If you're a woman who identifies with that sentiment – who spins along on an endless loop of activity dedicated to a single purpose but has yet to attract any hint of the thing she so longs to achieve – then the following section is for you.

Barbara's Story

Barbara, an assistant professor of Communications, always felt she missed her true calling – as a writer. She'd been writing ever since she was a child, but whatever she produced was stuffed in a drawer. This time, though, Barbara had a surefire idea for a story, something truly unique. This time she decided to go for broke. Her idea was for a children's book, and she was burning to get it down on paper. When she sat down to begin, the words flowed, driven by her excitement. She felt what Einstein must have felt churning out the Theory of Relativity. When she finished, she gathered her courage and set out in search of a publisher, one that would see the great potential of her book and market it on a wide scale. Barbara made a list of publishers and chose the one she thought most suitable. Trembling with nervous anticipation, she sent off the manuscript and waited for a reply (a positive one, of course). She couldn't sleep, and she lost her appetite. The only thing on her mind was reading the publisher's enthusiastic response, and she knew that the minute she did she'd be the happiest person on earth. After several nerve-wracking months, the precious envelope finally arrived. Her hand shaking, Barbara tore it open. Her eyes darted over the lines, all the way to the bottom of the page: "Thank you for sending your manuscript. Unfortunately, we find that it does not suit our needs. Best wishes in your future endeavors..."

Barbara was stunned. Tears poured from her eyes, and she was overtaken with a sense of despair. With whatever strength she could muster, she sent the manuscript to another publisher. And again, the scene replayed itself – a negative response and a gush of tears.

Barbara then entered an endless loop of activity, sending off copies of the manuscript to publisher after publisher. By the time she finished, 20 children's book publishers had received a copy. Every single one of them sent a rejection letter. Barbara nearly stopped functioning at the university and at home. Her children sensed the change, and they knew their mother's concerns were not with them. In fact, their mother's true concern was to bring another child into the world – her children's book. Until that time, she had no interest in socializing, felt no need to relax and go on a family vacation. She was totally preoccupied with thought of getting a positive response to her book. In the meantime, she was in agony. Her heart dropped every time she saw a new children's book in the stores; it was supposed to be hers, her book. She blanketed herself in self-pity, became obsessed with publishers, and tortured herself by asking, "Why me? Why is this happening to me?"

For you, Barbara, and for all you women who are or have been in a similar situation – longing for a dream that refuses to come true – I would like to share a very simple theory that is contained in a single phrase, just a few words that happen to carry a world of meaning: "The art of letting go."

Just... let go. Sometimes, just saying those two words to my coachees evokes a huge sigh of relief. Just let it loose. First of all, let yourself loose. Free yourself of your expectations, your disappointments, and everything wrapped up in them. Let up on the reins. If it happens, it happens. That would be fine. But if it doesn't happen, there will always be other avenues, other alternatives. Sometimes it's best to re-script the dream itself. Don't lose proportions. Take a deep breath and let go! What I'm advising is to liberate yourself and tame your obsession.

Only when you relax will you have the ability to attract anything positive into your life.

The art of letting go enables the Law of Attraction to bring your desires into your life in its own time, place, and manner. Letting go doesn't mean getting second best. It allows the Law of Attraction to realize your dream – or a variation of it – in the best way possible.

Is there something you're not attracting because you're trying so hard, or insisting that it come in a particular way or at a particular time? Let it go. Trust the Law of Attraction to bring it to you at the perfect time and in the perfect way.

Remember that some things take time. There's no way of being certain when it will come, or where or how. You simply have to accept the fact that it will happen at the right time. If you've reached the optimal state of relaxation, it surely won't be long. All you need to do is wait patiently and go whichever way the universe is flowing. If you can ride the waves of change that are bound to come as part of the process, everything will work out for the best.

And now, for the million dollar question: "When should I let go? How will I know when the time comes to relax a bit and shift to a lower gear?" The answer, according to the Art of Letting Go, is very simple: Let go when the price you are paying gets too high! Let go when you've done everything you can and you're beginning to get carried away. Let go when your NAFs start going wild. And, most importantly, let go when you find you've stopped paying attention to all those flowers at the roadside, and the only thing on your mind is that destination you're headed for. Take it easy, and bring back the smile to your face.

It's an old saying: *"Who is that enemy riding on my back, if not me, riding on myself?"* (unknown source).

4. Celebrate being active

The fourth way to help us overcome our inactivity and to spring into action is to celebrate our activity, in the true sense of the word.

The very fact that we are taking ourselves in hand, deciding to do something with our lives, taking initiative and showing responsibility is a great achievement for us. And as the old saying goes: *"If I don't do something for myself, who will do it for me?"* We should pat ourselves on the back every time we take a step in the right direction, and every time we take action to fulfill our Inner Core and silence our NAFs. We must share our progress with those closest to us, and accept their praise and compliments joyfully.

But, of course, we are not going to settle merely for a pat on the back; we are going to organize a real celebration, with prizes! We've got to celebrate the moment we began attracting what we've been working so hard to attain and have been seeking for so long – even if that success is quite small. Every time we feel we have successfully stepped out of our comfort zone and achieved something we previously considered taboo, we are going to treat ourselves to a little present – a new item of clothing, a meal in a restaurant, a good book, a pampering massage or just a brilliant smile at ourselves in the mirror.

- When we say "No!" to a friend who continually exploits our friendship we will celebrate our first victory over our **Please Everybody NAF**.

- When we sign up to study something new, we will celebrate our first victory over our **"I am Worthless" NAF**.

- When we finally allow our youngest child to have his first spiky haircut, and bid farewell to his golden baby curls, we will celebrate our first victory over our **Controllus NAF**.

- The first time we open our mouths to speak a foreign language, even though we're not fluent, we will celebrate our first victory over our **Failure NAF**.

- When we sign up for an art class, despite our many obligations – home, work, children etc – we will celebrate our first victory over our **Pressure NAF**.

- When we allow ourselves a piece of cake, in spite of our "permanent diet," we will celebrate our first victory over our **Fatso NAF**.

- When we stand by our opinion in a heated argument, we will celebrate our first victory over our **"What Will They Say?" NAF**.

- When we go for a routine checkup to the doctor's office without imagining the worst possible outcome – we will celebrate our first victory over our **Malignant NAF**.

In addition, we can keep reminding ourselves that we have good reason to celebrate by making frequent use of any of these phrases:

- "I did it!"
- "It all happened because of me."
- "I made progress, and I succeeded."
- "I was just burning to do it, and I got results."
- "It came to me because I was using my ability to attract."

And so on, and so forth, until activity and stepping out of our comfort zone become automatic actions which do not involve us being scared to the point of NAFness and paralysis.

And now, as promised, my tips for Code No. 6 — Spring into Action

Tip 1 – Do "the opposite"

Any time you feel depressed, angry, or stressed (which happens to all of us), just do the opposite.

What do I mean by this?

Wear your nicest clothes and best makeup, smile, wish everybody a cheery "Good morning," laugh out loud. Then watch your mood improve and the clouds disperse. Your demon may not be so terrible. You'll start projecting positive vibes and attracting the good things that make you feel happy and relaxed, after all.

Tip 2 – Maximize Your time – Make a time pie chart

Too often we rely on an age-old excuse for failing to do something: "I didn't have the time."

Your daily routine is probably jam-packed, and the following tip might help you organize the mess a bit.

Draw a pie chart divided into twenty-four segments, each segment representing an hour of the day.

On a separate sheet of paper, divide your daily routine into different categories, for example: children, partner, work, sleep, chores, leisure activities, telephone calls, friends, sport, hobbies, etc.

After you've completed the list of categories, go back to the pie chart and work out how many hours of each day you spend on each. Use a different color for each category to fill in as many segments as needed. For example:

Work –   9 hours: 9 segments

Sleep –   7 hours: 7 segments

Children – 4 hours: 4 segments

Carry on until you've filled in all the segments. Now all that remains is to check to see how you divide your time in the course of a day. Is it balanced? Do you spend too much time in one area at the expense of another? Do you leave enough time for yourself, or for hobbies?

Now prepare another, more balanced, chart. And don't just settle for a drawing. Try putting it into practice.

You'll be surprised to discover that even though time is a precious commodity, it is actually quite flexible and can be divided in ways that suit your desires and values.

Tip 3 – Compose mantras that will help you spring into action

Once we've decided to spring into action to achieve our goals and attract what we truly desire into our lives, a mantra may help give us a running start as we begin the process. Here are some suggestions for creating one of your own:

1. The mantra should be recited in the present tense, as if you've already achieved your ambition: "I'm wearing a size 8, and I feel wonderful," "I've got lots of clients, and it's so satisfying," "I'm getting along great with my coworkers."

2. Be sure the mantra you choose really makes you feel good. You may have decided to go on a diet and chosen the mantra, "I'm thin, and I feel great." But reciting it only makes you depressed because you can't really believe what you're saying. In that case, change the mantra to one that's better suited to your personality and makes you feel good.

   Remember: the law of attraction reacts to vibes that you send out. If you don't believe your own mantra, you'll be projecting your doubts, and you'll fail to attract what really want.

3. Your mantra can relate directly to the process you're going through. "I'm in the process of marketing my business," or "I'm working on improving my relationship with my children, and I'm starting to see results."

P.S. Now that you've cracked Code No. 6 – Spring Into Action, don't forget to open the accompanying workbook to the sixth chapter and pamper yourself with some more "attractive" exercises!

ᴇPILOGUE

As you read this book, you joined me on a special journey toward mastering the art of the law of attraction and becoming acquainted with the six codes. My aim was to share practical ways of dealing with the negative voices in our minds and attracting the things we truly desire into our lives.

Let's recap the codes we've cracked ...

Code No. 1 – Identification - taught us to identify our negative voices (our NAFs, Negative Attraction Factors), which attract the things we don't want into our lives. We learned to identify the vibes we send out at any given moment in order to attract the reality we desire.

Code No. 2 – Find Your Inner Core - helped us discover the most important things in our lives (our passions, loves, and personal values) and how these can serve as a magnet that attracts what we truly want and makes us more attractive as a result.

Code No. 3 – The Power of Thought - showed us how to direct our thoughts in positive directions, neutralize "stifling thoughts," and practice generating "enabling thoughts" that create a positive reality – all with the aim of attracting the things we desire.

Code No. 4 – Listen to Your Body - taught us to pay attention to what our body is telling us, involve our body in our decision-making, and trust our intuition in order to enhance our ability to attract what we truly desire in our lives.

Code No. 5 – Your Environment - taught us how great an influence our environment has upon us. We learned how to eliminate environmental factors that feed our NAFs and how to introduce elements in our lives that pull us upward and support us as we set out to discover what lies within our Inner Core.

Code No. 6 – Spring Into Action - urged us to step out of our comfort zone, break old habits, and start taking action in order to attract the reality we long for.

You'll soon be on your way to dealing with your NAFs - your negative voices and attracting the reality you long for, the things you truly desire!

On the upcoming pages you'll find the workbook for you to practice the six codes.

Remember, it all depends on you. You can do it if you really want to!!!

We, as women - we can do it if we want to!!!

"Remember, Ginger Rogers did everything Fred Astaire did, but she did it back wards and in high heels..."

— FAITH WHITTLESEY

Women, Decode the Law of Attraction Workbook

Crack the 6 codes:

How to THINK, ACT & ATTRACT
what you really want from life!

Orly Katz, MBA
Life, Business & Career
Coach for Women

And for Dessert – The Icing on the Cake

WOMEN, DECODE THE LAW OF ATTRACTION WORKBOOK

Women, Decode the Law Of Attraction Workbook helps you put the six codes into action. This 55-page workbook supplements the **Action Steps** in the book with a host of additional questions, exercises and assessments, and provides plenty of space for your responses and personal thoughts.

As you read the book, you joined me on a special journey toward mastering the art of the law of attraction and becoming acquainted with the six codes. My aim was to share practical ways of dealing with the negative voices in our minds and of attracting the things we truly desire into our lives.

In this workbook, which I view as the dessert course, I've got a lovely bowl of cherries waiting for you. Each cherry has more exercises (in addition to the exercises written in the book) to reinforce the codes. These cherries/exercises are my gift to you to set you on your way. I hope these little morsels will motivate you and serve as a reminder, reinforcing the material covered in my book. Treat yourself to a real bowl of cherries as you perform these exercises. Make sure that you relish every bite of each juicy cherry you pop in your mouth. Savor the juiciness and remember that our aim is to add more cherries to the whipped cream of our lives. Cherries are juicy and sweet, but they can also be slightly tart. We can't remove the tartness, but we can do our best to extract all the juice we can so that we're sure to get the sweetness as well.

So, happy guzzling, and "Bon Appétit"!

You'll soon be on your way to dealing with your NAFs - your negative voices - and attracting the reality you long for, the things you truly desire!

THE FIRST CHERRY

CRACKING CODE No. 1 - IDENTIFICATION

Identifying your NAFs in Your Personal and Professional Life (NAF = Negative Attraction Factor)

	The dominant NAFs in my personal life	The dominant NAFs in my career and my path to self-fulfillment
Names of the NAFs	1. 2. 3.	1. 2. 3.
What they tell me	1. 2. 3.	1. 2. 3.
How this affects my actions	1. 2. 3.	1. 2. 3.

The Melody of Life

This exercise will help you discover what you project in every area of your life, what vibes you're sending out, and how your NAFs prevent you from attracting the results you want. In other words, it will let you know the areas in which you should deliberately put the Law of Attraction into effect.

The name of the exercise implies that our lives are composed of different keys, just like the keys of a piano that create either a harmonious and pleasant melody or a discordant and unbearable noise. We have the right and power to decide which type of melody we'd like to play, and to turn the out-of-tune noises into beautiful tunes.

1. Draw a set of piano keys on a sheet of paper. Label each key with a different aspect of your life: partnership, parenthood, family, career, physical fitness, fun, friends, hobbies, health, etc. Write down only the aspects that relate to your own life.

2. Now, on a scale of zero to 10, estimate your level of satisfaction with your functioning in these areas and the results it has brought. Zero represents a total lack of satisfaction and 10 a complete sense of satisfaction.

3. Draw a horizontal line across each key to indicate the score you gave. Now color the area above each line in black. If, for example, you rated your "career" category 4, indicating you are not very satisfied with this aspect of your life, you would leave the area from zero to 4 white and color the rest of the key black. Now your drawing really resembles a piano keyboard.

4. Next, your job is to see where the white parts of the keys are high enough (above 7) to indicate that you're satisfied with your functioning in that area. Similarly, take a look at where black is the predominant color. This is where our NAFs and their effect on the Law of Attraction come into the picture. For the keys with a score of 7 or lower, your NAFs are at work, turning your melody of life into an awful screech. They're manipulating you, convincing you that your best bet is to dance to the music they're playing. But, in reality, your inability to act, caused by the NAFs, sends out negative vibes and prevents you from attracting the outcomes you want. That is why you feel dissatisfied, as if you've missed out on something good. For the keys with a score above 7, you've let the positive, optimistic sounds ring forth, and, as a result, you've attracted what you desired.

5. It's time now to draw the appropriate conclusions. In which areas should you try to raise your score? These areas will become your top priority. It is in these areas that you want to identify your NAFs. What are they telling you, and how do they affect you? Try to determine what benefit lies behind each of the NAFs, as opposed to the benefit of applying the Identification Code, while paying attention to the other voices in your head - the optimistic ones.

6. Make a decision and... good luck!

Identify where you're stuck with Your Life at the Moment?

		Never 0	Hardly ever 1	Some-times 2	Always 3
1	I feel bad just thinking about getting out of bed in the morning and going to work.				
2	After getting together with friends, I return home with an unpleasant feeling in my stomach.				
3	I feel I'm capable of lots more professionally, but I don't take the initiative.				
4	I spend so little time thinking about myself that I don't know what things are good for me in life.				
5	My partner deflates every idea/ suggestion/initiative I have and restrains me from acting.				
6	My "to do" list follows me everywhere and gives me no rest.				
7	I worry a lot about not investing enough in my children.				
8	I wake up in the middle of the night worrying about money.				
9	When people tell me I look good, I don't believe them.				
10	I try new diets, but nothing helps.				
11	I try in vain to get my husband to understand me.				
12	I don't like sharing my successes with my friends because they don't hand out praise.				
13	I don't manage to treat myself to quiet time for me alone.				

		Never 0	Hardly ever 1	Some- times 2	Always 3
14	It seems like a miracle if we manage to get through a month without going into debt.				
15	For years, I've wanted to move to a new house or apartment but can't seem to do it.				
16	I could kick myself for not being able to quit smoking.				
17	I don't know how to set limits for my children.				
18	When I get a sudden urge to do something nice for myself, I quickly bury the idea.				
19	I don't exercise, and that really bothers my conscience.				
20	I envy people whose home is their castle. I don't feel that way about my home.				

Purpose of the questionnaire:

1. Identify the current, real situation in every aspect of your life.

2. Get some idea of the ideal situation. In which areas should you begin to make changes to raise your level of satisfaction?

Analyzing the responses:

1. Look at each area of your life separately.

2. Total the points for each of these areas.

Identify the areas in which you are not satisfied, according to the following chart:

Area	Question #s	Points for each question	Total points for area
Time for myself	6, 13		
My partner	5, 11		
Personal development	4, 18		
Friends	2, 12		
Children	7, 17		
Health	16, 19		
Career	1, 3		
Money	8, 14		
Living conditions	15, 20		
Body and appearance	9, 10		

What three areas have the highest number of total points?

1. _____

2. _____

3. _____

Those are the 3 areas in which you're stuck in your life at this moment (and are attracting what you don't want, instead of what you want).

Daily NAF Monitoring

Design a table for noting all the NAFs that spring to mind during the course of a week.

What things did you attract into your life at those times (your real situation)?

What are you interested in attracting in this specific field (you ideal situation)?

Name of my NAF	What did I Attract?	What am I interested to attract?

You are not the only "lucky one" with your NAF

This exercise will help you to realize and understand just how widespread the NAF phenomenon is. You are not the only person with a NAF. Everyone around you has them.

Over the next week, listen carefully to the people around you: your partner, children, friends, colleagues etc. Notice how many times their NAF speaks for them out of their mouths. You might hear things like:

"I just can't take it any more…"

"I have to do it, but I really don't want to."

"I feel awkward."

"What will she think of me?"

"I'm no good at that…"

Notice how the NAF influences their emotions and their actions.

The person	Name of the NAF	What did the person say?	What was the influence?

THE SECOND CHERRY

CRACKING CODE NO. 2 – FIND YOUR INNER CORE

When Was The Last Time You Put Yourself in the Center?

- When was the last time you did something entirely for yourself?

_____

_____

_____

_____

_____

_____

- What was it?

_____

_____

_____

_____

_____

_____

_____

_____

- How will you give yourself permission to put yourself in the center?

  _____

  _____

  _____

  _____

  _____

  _____

- How possible is it, in your view, to commit to something meant only for you?

  _____

  _____

  _____

  _____

  _____

  _____

  _____

- If there were suddenly an opportunity to do something you've dreamed about, would you jump at it or let it pass by?

  _____

  _____

  _____

  _____

  _____

  _____

A Blast from the Past

Each new decision we make in our lives is a difficult process.

This exercise will help you see if your decision making process was influenced by one of your **NAFs** rather than your **Inner Core**.

- What was the issue you were debating about?

_____

_____

_____

_____

_____

_____

_____

_____

- See which values were ranked low on your Valuemeter. Try to remember the decisions you made in the past that led you into these sorts of situations?

_____

_____

_____

_____

_____

_____

_____

_____

_____

- Which were the options you didn't choose? The options that, had you chosen them, might have allowed your most important values to be better represented?

  _____

  _____

  _____

  _____

  _____

  _____

  _____

- Think about the role your NAF played in your decision-making process. What did it tell you?

  _____

  _____

  _____

  _____

  _____

  _____

- Who had more influence over your decision, your Inner Core or your NAF?

  _____

  _____

  _____

  _____

  _____

  _____

Looking into the Future

- Think about a decision you are mulling over right now:

  _____

  _____

  _____

  _____

  _____

  _____

  _____

- Write down what the different voices in your head are saying about it:

  _____

  _____

  _____

  _____

  _____

  _____

  _____

- Study your Valuemeter: your top 5 values are:

  _____

  _____

  _____

  _____

  _____

  _____

  _____

- Think about which option you would like to raise on the Valuemeter:

_____

_____

_____

_____

_____

_____

- Recognize the voice of your NAF:

_____

_____

_____

_____

_____

- Remember the Identification Code, and the importance of focusing on your Inner Core, and… decide.

What is your decision?

_____

_____

_____

_____

_____

_____

Mapping Your Dreams

"A man is not old until regrets take the place of dreams."

— JOHN BARRYMORE

One of the most effective ways to make something happen is to imagine it clearly, as though it were really happening. Visualize it in front of your eyes as realistically as possible. Remember it, engrave it on your memory. This is an excellent way to keep ourselves from being carried away by life's daily routine. One pleasant way to go about this is to map out your dreams. A "dream map" is a collage that you create to illustrate the things you want to achieve.

1. Equip yourself with a large sheet of construction paper, old magazines, scissors, glue, felt tip pens and a lot of creativity.

2. The object of the exercise is to design a map featuring all the things you want in your life. Leaf through the magazines, and each time that you find an attractive picture cut it out and glue it to your map. You can also add inspirational slogans and catchphrases.

3. Place your map in a prominent location, somewhere you'll see it every day, and try to imagine what life would be like if all the dreams came true. If, for example, you wished for a baby, imagine yourself taking a baby for a walk in the stroller on a Saturday morning. Imagine what it would be wearing, think about its cute smile, imagine the reactions of passersby etc. Carry on and imagine the details of each picture on your map - the things most important to you - as though they really existed. You'll be surprised to learn how much strength this visualization will give you as you try to fulfill your dreams.

THE THIRD CHERRY

Cracking Code No. 3 – The Power of Thought

Your Home Movie Center

- What types of scenarios are usually projected in your mind?

  _____

  _____

  _____

  _____

  _____

  _____

  _____

- When was the last time you projected a horror movie in your mind?

  _____

  _____

  _____

  _____

  _____

  _____

  _____

- When was the last time you projected a movie with a happy ending? What was in the movie, and how did the real-life situation end?

_____

_____

_____

_____

_____

_____

_____

- Are you facing a stressful task of any kind? If so, what is it?

_____

_____

_____

_____

_____

_____

_____

- Are you willing to make a commitment to project a positive mental scenario?

_____

_____

_____

_____

_____

_____

_____

- Describe your scenario in detail, just as it will appear on your home movie center.

  _____

  _____

  _____

  _____

  _____

  _____

  _____

  _____

  _____

Enter your Zen

- When was the last time you concentrated solely on an activity in which you were engaged?

_____

_____

_____

_____

_____

_____

- What was the activity?

_____

_____

_____

_____

_____

_____

- Is this something you do daily, or was it a one-time activity?

_____

_____

_____

_____

_____

_____

_____

- Are there other activities on which you devote all your attention, without thinking about the results, the surroundings, your debts, or anything else?

_____

_____

_____

_____

_____

_____

- Are you willing to make the commitment to bringing these sorts of activities into your life, on a frequent basis?

_____

_____

_____

_____

_____

_____

An Ounce of Prevention

- When was the last time you spent the night tossing and turning, unable to sleep because you were plagued by worries?

_____

_____

_____

_____

_____

_____

_____

- What was worrying you?

_____

_____

_____

_____

_____

- What "cure" can you prepare in advance? That is, something else to think about to channel your mind in a different direction - a positive one.

_____

_____

_____

_____

_____

- Make a list of all the pleasant topics (cures) you can think about the moment your NAFs pop up to plague you.

_____

_____

_____

_____

_____

_____

Identify Stifling Thoughts

In the following chart of stifling thoughts, try to come up with the false assumption on which each is based. (In some cases, the same false assumption may apply to different thoughts.)

After you've written them all down, do a self-analysis to think of questions you might ask yourself to help you counter these stifling thoughts. The exercise is directly relevant to your life. It will help you understand how stifling thoughts affect the other thoughts you have, particularly the enabling thoughts that generate positive reality. You'll also practice moving the beam of light from your stifling thoughts to your enabling thoughts.

Type of Stifling Thought	Explanation	False Assumption	Questions to ask yourself
A stifling thought that prevents change	A thought that makes us oppose or fear change	(Example) It's possible to find stability in this world	1. When was the last time I faced a change and tried with all my might to avoid making it? 2. What was the last time I changed anything, and what were the results?
A stifling thought that represses feelings	A thought that keeps us from fully feeling and experiencing things		
A stifling thought that leads us to be judgmental	A thought that makes us particularly critical of people we know		

Type of Stifling Thought	Explanation	False Assumption	Questions to ask yourself
A stifling thought that ignores the present	A thought that prevents us from living in the present		
A stifling thought that limits development	A thought that keeps us from expressing ourselves and growing		
A stifling thought that compels results	A thought that convinces us our actions will have only one inevitable result		
A stifling thought that disregards other perspectives	A thought that does not allow us to see different perspectives		
A stifling thought that restricts beliefs	This type of thought leads us to believe that taking a particular course of action will produce only one possible result.		
A stifling thought that exaggerates what others tell us	A thought that leads us to respond in an exaggerated fashion to the things people tell us.		
Other stifling thoughts			

Identify the Beliefs that Prevent you from Acting

- Think about things you believe that prevent you from taking certain actions.

_____

_____

_____

_____

_____

_____

_____

- On what false assumptions are these beliefs based?

_____

_____

_____

_____

_____

_____

- What do you have to gain by holding these beliefs?

_____

_____

_____

_____

_____

_____

- **What do you have to lose?**

_____

_____

_____

_____

_____

_____

_____

- **How can you counter them?**

_____

_____

_____

_____

_____

_____

_____

- **What is the first thing you'll do to deal with them?**

_____

_____

_____

_____

_____

_____

_____

- **When will you start?**

  _____

  _____

  _____

  _____

  _____

  _____

  _____

- **What mantras can you recite to help rid yourself of these beliefs and turn your stifling thoughts into enabling thoughts?**

  _____

  _____

  _____

  _____

  _____

  _____

  _____

THE FOURTH CHERRY

CRACKING CODE No. 4 - LISTEN TO YOUR BODY

How to Use your Body in the Decision-Making Process?

1. Clearly define the factors that are hindering your decision-making process.

2. Arrange for a relaxing atmosphere: make sure the house is quiet, lie down in a darkened room with nothing to disturb you.

3. Breathe in deeply several times to relax yourself, then commence the process.

4. Imagine yourself having chosen the first option. What are you doing? What are you wearing? How do you act? Think about all the good things that will result from this option, ignore the negative aspects, and don't think about the second option.

5. Concentrate on the physical sensations and pay attention to how you feel. You can use images, feelings, emotions, anything that works. You can describe your sensations as if you were an object or a child, for instance.

6. Now imagine yourself in the second situation, having chosen the second option. What are you doing? What are you wearing? How do you act? Again, you must only think

about the good things that will result from this option; ignore the negative aspects, and don't think about the first option.

7. Concentrate on your physical sensations and how you feel this time. Again, image, feelings, and emotions are all acceptable tools.

8. Make your decision, smile, and pamper yourself with a massage, you deserve it!

How to Identify Your Intuition?

- When was the last time you acted according to your intuition?

_____

_____

_____

_____

_____

_____

_____

- What was the occasion?

_____

_____

_____

_____

_____

_____

_____

- What were the results?

_____

_____

_____

_____

_____

_____

_____

- How did your intuition make itself known?

  _____

  _____

  _____

  _____

  _____

  _____

  _____

- What did you feel at the time?

  _____

  _____

  _____

  _____

  _____

  _____

  _____

- Did your intuition ever reappear?

  _____

  _____

  _____

  _____

  _____

  _____

  _____

- If so, when did this happen, and how did it make itself known in each case?

  _____

  _____

  _____

  _____

  _____

  _____

  _____

  _____

- Do you see any pattern in the circumstances in which your intuition appears?

  _____

  _____

  _____

  _____

  _____

  _____

  _____

  _____

How Can Your Intuition Tell You If the Guy You Met is the Right One for You?

The object of this exercise is to neutralize the noises that our NAF is making and learn how to identify our intuition, awaken it, listen to it, summon it when needed, and rely on it for information. If you've met a guy and want to clarify your feeling about him: Is he loyal? Can you trust him? Is he reliable? try this:

1. Imagine that your car breaks down in the middle of the night and you call him for help. (Of course, you can imagine any such situation that comes to mind.)

2. Try to imagine what his reaction might be. Is it, "I'm on my way?" Or is he searching around for excuses? Maybe he'll settle for giving you instructions over the phone.

3. In situations like this, rational thinking is useless. Our intellect can't tell us what will happen. You're only imaging the scenario, but your gut feeling is telling you much more, based on his tone of voice or the course of action he chooses.

4. Make a decision, and be confident that it was the right one for you.

THE FIFTH CHERRY

CRACKING CODE NO. 5 -YOUR ENVIRONMENT

Assertiveness, or How to say "No" Nicely

- When do you feel uncomfortable saying "No"?

_____

_____

_____

_____

_____

_____

- Who is involved in these situations? (family, friends, spouse, children, colleagues, boss, etc.)

_____

_____

_____

_____

_____

- When do you feel comfortable saying "No"? To whom?

  _____

  _____

  _____

  _____

  _____

  _____

  _____

- What is the worse thing that will happen if you say "No"?

  _____

  _____

  _____

  _____

  _____

  _____

  _____

  _____

- What have you got to gain by saying "No"?

  _____

  _____

  _____

  _____

  _____

  _____

  _____

- Start practicing: To whom will you say "No" this week and live to tell the tale?

_____

_____

_____

_____

_____

_____

_____

_____

_____

Identify the Energy Drainers in Every Area of Your Life

1. Categorize the different areas of your life. For example, marriage, children, parents, career/job, friends, exercise, health, money, etc.

2. For each category, identify one thing that bothers you enough to work toward changing it.

3. Decide what you need to do to complete the unfinished business at hand.

4. Set priorities for each category.

5. Set a schedule.

6. Fill in the information in the chart below.

7. Just begin.

Good luck!

	What disturbs me?	What will I do to change things?	My priorities	Schedule	Monitoring the results	How do I feel now? (after the change)
Spouse or partner						
Children						
Relatives						
Work						
Colleagues						
Friends						
Spare time						
House or apartment						
Physical exercise						
Hobbies						
Health						
Money						

The Things I'm Thankful For

"The talent for being happy is appreciating and liking what you have, instead of what you don't have."

– WOODY ALLEN

Too many times, we see the things we don't have, the things that bother us, and the things that are "wrong" with us. We never notice all the good things that we already have in our lives, the things we take for granted.

1. Prepare a diary or notebook with an attractive cover.

2. Make a list of the things for which you are grateful for in your life - the things that are unique to you, things you would not be prepared to give up at any price, things you worked hard to achieve but sometimes forget just how good they make you feel.

3. Make yourself a new routine. Every night before you go to bed, take your diary and note three things that happened that day for which you are grateful. They can be little things, like that wonderful conversation you had with your young son, or an interesting book you read, or, of course, bigger, more dramatic things.

4. If you don't feel like writing them down, just think about them before you drift off to sleep. You'll be surprised to find yourself falling asleep with a smile on your face.

THE SIXTH CHERRY

CRACKING CODE NO. 6 - SPRING INTO ACTION

Which Habits Should I Change?

- What is the deepest-seated habit in your life, the one with the greatest effect on your daily life?

_____

_____

_____

_____

_____

_____

_____

- What do you gain by performing this habit?

_____

_____

_____

_____

_____

_____

- **What do you lose by performing this habit?**

_____

_____

_____

_____

_____

_____

_____

- **What do you need to do to break the habit?**

_____

_____

_____

_____

_____

_____

_____

- **What is the first thing you'll do to break the habit?**

_____

_____

_____

_____

_____

_____

_____

- And now the commitment: When will you take this first step?

  _____

  _____

  _____

  _____

  _____

  _____

  _____

  _____

Failure – That's the Whole Story?

- What was your first painful failure in life?

_____

_____

_____

_____

_____

_____

_____

- How did you feel?

_____

_____

_____

_____

_____

_____

_____

- What did you do afterward?

_____

_____

_____

_____

_____

_____

_____

• What were the results of your actions?

_____

_____

_____

_____

_____

_____

_____

_____

• Did you ever give up after failing at anything? Describe the incident.

_____

_____

_____

_____

_____

_____

_____

_____

• What was the greatest lesson you ever learned after failing?

_____

_____

_____

_____

_____

_____

_____

- Have you ever had occasion to believe that "failure is a challenge on the way to success?" If so, describe the incident. How did you act, and what was the success that followed your actions?

  _____

  _____

  _____

  _____

  _____

  _____

  _____

Identify What You're Chasing, or How to Practice the Art of Letting Go

Try to give honest answers to the following:

1. Define what you're chasing, what's chasing you, and what you should let go of:

   _____

   _____

   _____

   _____

2. What are your NAFs telling you to do?

   _____

   _____

   _____

   _____

3. What have you got to gain from this chase?

   _____

   _____

   _____

   _____

4. What have you got to lose from the chase?

   _____

   _____

   _____

   _____

5. Describe the emptiness you expect to follow the letting go process.

_____

_____

_____

_____

6. How do you think you can fill that emptiness?

_____

_____

_____

_____

7. How do you think you might change, adjust, or define your dream differently as a means of attracting what you really want?

_____

_____

_____

_____

Your Dream Can Come True...

- What dream have you've decided to focus on at the moment?

  _____

  _____

  _____

  _____

- List five things, large or small, that you will do in the coming month to help your dream become a reality

1. _____

   _____

2. _____

   _____

3. _____

   _____

4. _____

   _____

5. _____

   _____

And now, of course, your commitment:

I, _____ will make the following change:

_____ by _____ (date)

because changing my life depends on me!

Signed: _____

Success Scrapbook

"Nothing builds self-esteem and self confidence like accomplishment."

– Thomas Carlyle

Wouldn't it be nice if you had a personal scrapbook to record all of the successes and golden moments in your past, something to keep you going during rough times when you're filled with self-doubt and your NAF starts to rear its ugly head? I invite you to take a blast into the past and dig out some souvenirs to keep you going in the present.

A success scrapbook or album is a documentary record that provides evidence of your success.

You can include the list of your good qualities and your strong points that you prepared in Chapter 2, references from former employers, love letters, synopses of successful projects at work, pictures of your children, partner, or home – anything that fills you with feelings of warmth and pride, and, most importantly, chases your NAF away and makes room for the really important things in your life.

My Attraction Diary

Many times, we see only what is negative – the things we fail to achieve. We sense we are victims, and this prevents us from realizing our ability to attract anything positive.

1. Get a small notebook. Decorate it any way you like.

2. Write down all the things you succeeded in attracting to yourself in a day, even the most minor things.

3. Write down what you did in order to attract these things.

4. Note how you celebrated attracting these things.

5. Start a new routine: Every night before you go to sleep, write down at least three things that you succeeded in attracting that day.

Don't forget:

"It is inevitable when one has a great need of something, one finds it. What you need you attract to you like a lover."

– GERTRUDE STEIN

Who is Orly Katz?

Orly Katz, MBA is a leading international expert in women's coaching. She is a dynamic, engaging speaker and a highly sought-after Life, Business and Career Coach. Orly has the talent and the ability to inform and inspire audiences toward finding their direction, balance and satisfaction in their lives and careers. As the founder of O.K. Coaching – The Women's Coaching Center, she guides and coaches thousands of women. Orly also lectures, moderates workshops and conducts group coaching for executives, business owners, large organizations and private sector groups wishing to improve their life's balance, marketing and management skills.

Married and a mother of three, Orly is a regularly featured speaker for professional associations, academic institutes, government agencies, sales organizations and corporations. The 6 Codes of the Law of Attraction, developed in the book, are the codes she uses in her lectures, workshops and coaching sessions. She is often a featured speaker on television shows, radio, internet and newspapers in which she discusses coaching issues relevant to women and working mothers.

Orly, born in Haifa, Israel, has a PCC (Professional Certified Coach) accredited Coaching Diploma from the ICF (International Coach Federation). She is a graduate of the prestigious College of Executive Coaching in the U.S., and of the Life Coaching Institute program. A qualified food engineer, Orly graduated the Technion (Israel's premier institute of technology) and holds an MBA. She received her certification as a group facilitator at Israel's Bar Ilan University, and she is a certified tutor in Creative Thinking, accredited by the Open University. In the past, Orly was a Marketing Manager at Unilever Israel.

Her first book "To Each her Own Dizzi" was published in Israel in 2005.

For further information about Orly's coaching programs, workshops, book, or to schedule her for a presentation, visit her website at:

www.okcoaching.com